S0-AEP-031

Defying
Autism

Defying
Autism

Karen Mayer Cunningham

CREATION
HOUSE
A STRANG COMPANY

DEFYING AUTISM by Karen Mayer Cunningham
Published by Creation House
A Strang Company
600 Rinehart Road
Lake Mary, Florida 32746
www.creationhouse.com

This book or parts thereof may not be reproduced in any
form, stored in a retrieval system, or transmitted in any
form by any means—electronic, mechanical, photocopy,
recording, or otherwise—without prior written permission of
the publisher, except as provided by United States of America
copyright law.

Unless otherwise noted, all Scripture quotations are from
New International Version of the Bible. Copyright © 1973,
1978, 1984, International Bible Society. Used by permission.

Design Director: Bill Johnson

Copyright © 2008 by Karen Mayer Cunningham
All rights reserved

Library of Congress Control Number: 2008912231
International Standard Book Number: 978-1-59979-628-4

09 10 11 12 13 — 98765432
Printed in the United States of America

To all of you standing, hoping, and believing for your miraculous healing.

ACKNOWLEDGMENTS

- To Sheila Ramsey—mentor, leader, and prayer warrior: I thank you for laying your life down for our family.

- To my girlfriends: your love and support through this journey kept me focused. I am so blessed to have you in my life.

- To Sue Thompson: thank you for your golden pen. What an amazing writer you are.

- To my family: the Earls and the Cunninghams. Thank you, thank you, thank you.

- To my wonderful husband, Cortney, and my beautiful children, James, Paige, and Caden.

CONTENTS

1
SANTA ANA WINDS

I EXHALED AS I SETTLED into seat 12C and stared out
the window. I wasn't looking at anything in particular. I didn't feel like focusing. I closed my eyes and
fell asleep before the plane took off.

After a while, I awakened and looked around in an
attempt to distract myself from my own thoughts.
Couldn't see much of anything to warrant my interest,
so I was stuck, and here came the onslaught: what in the
world had been going on for the last four years of my
life? I thought Los Angeles was going to be the city of
angels. I had honestly expected it to be my city of dreams,
and I know what a cliché that is. It had turned out to be
more like the city of nightmares. It's a nightmare when
your hope goes unfulfilled. It was a nightmare for me to
have left Texas with the expectation of becoming famous
only to see virtually nothing happen. Oh, I know that
thousands, probably tens of thousands, show up in Los
Angeles each year expecting to make it in the entertainment industry by sheer force of undeniable talent, only
to hit a brick wall. My dream of making it diminished a

little more with every table I waited on. So many pointless jobs rolled into wasted years. I had hit that brick wall, and now here I was on a flight home to Austin, admitting defeat.

I had nothing to show for my time in Tinseltown. I had less in my bank account now than when I had moved West. I had gulped down my pride and asked my parents if I could move back in with them. My hopes for success were dried up, my biological clock was ticking and, to top it all off, I had gained weight and I knew this would be the first visible sign to everyone at home that I was returning a *loser*.

I felt each bump as the wheels of the plane touched down on the runway at Robert Mueller airport. Waves of depression overtook me, and that "everything is rotten" curtain descended upon my heart as I pulled my suitcases out of the baggage claim area. I didn't finish college so I had no degree. Any ambition I had owned was lost in Los Angeles. I didn't have a relationship with anyone. The only thing I had to show for my life was a shipment of boxes coming home by UPS Ground.

Dad was waiting for me. He opened his arms to hug me and I buried my face in his shoulder, but not before I saw the disappointment on his face. I knew that he was shocked at the amount of weight I had put on. It was one of the many side effects of "protecting" myself, but I didn't feel so protected right now.

I looked out the window as he drove and I worked to find a bright spot, anything, about coming home. Austin was so different from the world I had just left and I had almost forgotten what it was like to be home. The scenery was beautiful and spacious; there were more fields than buildings. More clear skies than pollution. More driving than just sitting in traffic. But Austin felt almost miniature compared to Los Angeles, which seems so much bigger than life the comparison was almost unfair. The cars we passed looked comically like Hot Wheels toys. My parents' house looked like a dollhouse, as I remembered some of the "McMansions" I had seen out West. I felt so disconnected and sad that it was hard to put on a face to greet my mother.

I had gone to Los Angeles to manage my own personal version of *American Idol.* I knew I had comedic talent, and I was determined to put myself in position to be one of the ones who made it in the brutal world of stand-up comedy. I thought I had what it took. Like so many, I really didn't understand how incredibly difficult it was to make it, not just in the arena of comedy clubs, but also in any aspect of the entertainment industry. I was disillusioned, depressed, and felt like a complete failure. I had started out with some big hopes and plans and had slowly compromised them right into the ground. I now had a past, and it wasn't a lovely picture. Like a cherry on top of a sundae of broken dreams, I was ashamed.

I had to get on my feet and begin my life back in Texas. My dad helped me to obtain a car and insurance, and I was fortunate enough to find work through a temporary staffing agency. Austin was not my idea of perfect, but in just a few days I was off to a fairly decent start. I began to take some deep breaths, reminding myself that maybe there is hope after a dream-killing crash. "God is still on the throne," we used to say in church. God wasn't exactly the center of my life, though, as I had displaced Him for my ambitions and expectations. I didn't think wearing God on my sleeve as I made the rounds in Los Angeles was a good idea. I loved to party, and I didn't think He'd want to boogie down at the many functions I frequented. Church life and God-talk was a part of my past, not a central focus of my ambitions.

But maybe it was time for me to come home in more ways than one. Maybe it would be a good idea to get back into church. That was the same thing as getting into God, right?

How fortuitous that my first Sunday back in Austin was Easter Sunday! But as Mom and Dad and I walked into Marshall Ford Baptist Church, I was hit again with a feeling of self-consciousness and humiliation. My weight gain was obvious to everyone, and folks at church had a special way of letting a person know they noticed. "Wow, Karen!" they'd say with big smiles on their faces and glances to my middle. "You look so... *different*." This is the comment you get from people who have not seen you in a while and want to tell you how much worse you look now than when you left. I forced a smile as I gave hugs and walked away from stares to my backside. I found a seat and squeezed into the pew.

"This will all be over in a couple of hours," I told myself as the lights went down. The Easter pageant was about to begin, and I tried to find comfort in the familiar. Lights go up! Music begins! Los Angeles it's not, but it's the best Texas Southern Baptists have to offer, and anyway...wait a minute! *Who is that guy?* The music leader was astonishingly good-looking! In that very moment, from the first second I saw him, I was drawn to him. As the drama began, I discovered the man was not only gorgeous, he also had an amazing voice. I started to feel really goofy. I couldn't stop staring at him, and luckily I didn't have to, since he was the center of attention.

When the musical ended, I was surprisingly disappointed. I gathered myself as though I were waking up from a dream and headed to Sunday school. I couldn't get over how fixated I was on that guy. I was so bothered by it. He works at a *church*! That didn't exactly fit into my party lifestyle. "Get real," I told myself. I had been staring at a little fantasy in the church cantata. No guarantees I had ever even be introduced to the man. "Remember how depressed you are? How worthless you feel? Back to reality."

I shook off thoughts of Mr. Good-Looking Music Leader as I entered the singles Sunday school class. I took a quick look around. There were about five other people seated around the room, but I was clearly the only one who had not been divorced or recently released from prison. I knew in my heart, though, that they looked down on me: being twenty-six and single in Texas is like having the plague. At least the ex-cons have an excuse for not being married: they'd been locked up. Could my life get any worse? I settled into a seat, so self-conscious I felt radioactive.

You know how some things just sound like a really good story that a fantastically creative person just made up? Maybe something like what I'm telling you now? Here is the honest truth: the teacher walked in and I looked up into the face of a change of fate—it was Mr. Good-Looking Music Leader! Life was immediately rosy and my eyes were glued to him as he led the class. Not only was he attractive, not only was he a great singer with an impressive command of a bunch of musicians, but I noticed he was book smart, calm, and patient. It also did not escape me that he came with a past: he had several phone calls from his children during the lesson, which told me he probably had an ex-wife somewhere (I could not bring myself to consider he might actually be married). In a very short time I had planned our lives together, but watching him blush as he apologized for the interruptions caused me to reconsider. I was pretty sure I didn't want to sign up for former spouse and kids. Nothing is as easy as it looks at first glance, is it?

Sunday school ended, and I walked out to the parking lot, still thinking of how Mr. Good-Looking Music Leader had captivated me, but I was feeling low. He could not possibly be my type. Funny how my dead-end years in Los Angeles suddenly made me far more sophisticated than a music leader in a Baptist church. I had been on the track to the big time! I had been to parties where really important people laughed at my jokes (and then ignored me, but that's not important right now) and long hours on the freeway had put me in Malibu and Beverly Hills and a lot of other places most people only see on television. That was the real world for me. What was I thinking?

I got in the truck with my parents and as I shut the door I opened my mouth. "I just want you guys to know that I would never, ever, ever marry some guy who worked at a church. I just wouldn't." My mom and dad, not anywhere as surprised as *I* was at what I had just blurted out, looked at each other and then at me. "OK, Karen," my mother said, looking sideways at my father. "Thank you for letting us know. We have no idea where that came from, but thank you." We drove home in silence, my emphatic pronouncement hanging in the air like an argument. No way, I thought. I have been places. No church-type for me.

Soon daily life found its rhythm and my natural self-confidence began to return. "I am still a young woman," I reminded myself. "I will figure something out." I was working as a receptionist at a title company by day and waitressing by night. You can imagine what these careers did for my dating life. It really didn't matter, though. As ticked-off as I had been that Sunday morning after the Easter program and the singles class, I was not interested in dating anyone but that breathtaking music leader, Tom Mayer. He was all I thought about. Forget visions of life in Los Angeles and my revulsion of guys who'd made church work a vocation. Anytime I had a moment to myself, his face seized my mind like a drug. How in the world did I go from near-suicidal despair to joyfully obsessive manhunting in such a short time?

Welcome to the effects of romantic attraction!

So I did what any smart woman in my particular situation would do: I joined the choir. How else was I supposed to spend time with Mr. Good-Looking Music Leader and not seem desperate or appear to be a stalker?

This decision opened up vast possibilities for me: I could flirt with him while seeming to be a dedicated churchgoer. I could act pushy, strong, and opinionated (which is kind of exactly how I am) to get him to notice me. I could play the funny, ditzy blonde to captivate his attention.

It got me nowhere. Tom didn't seem interested in that kind of behavior.

What to do? I studied the man, trying to figure out what might get his attention. I worked hard in choir practice. I asked somewhat intelligent questions ("Are we holding that beat on the last bar?"). I was a model soprano with a funny quip at just the right moment. I figured if I could get the whole group laughing, he'd have to notice I was worth a second look. Little by little, I chipped away at his blind eyes, willing him to acknowledge me. To my great satisfaction, we were soon doing the dance that people do when they like each other: compliments, smiles, gazes, group outings. Finally: the call. You know what I'm talking about. It's the one event that makes you say to yourself, "Oh yeah—he likes me."

"Hi Karen, this is Tom Mayer. I just wanted to call and give you the page numbers for choir practice on Wednesday night." *Right. The page numbers for choir practice.* Nobody else in the choir got this phone call. Who needed to know page numbers ahead of time? Oh yes, this was my signal to move forward, and I put my foot on the gas pedal with fixed determination.

Since Tom had two daughters who stayed with him every weekend, I created hanging-out time around their visits. I came up with a plan that allowed us all to be together in a family-like setting: I would pick up food and a movie on my way to his house so I could keep the girls fed and entertained while allowing a little time for the two of us to get to know each other. That was our dating life. We never called them dates, but who were we kidding? Dinner and a movie is a date! OK, there were kids present, but that's not especially significant. They were dates!

This is how we became acquainted, how we built our friendship. Maybe it wasn't the ideal situation, but by this time I had admitted what I knew from the moment I first set eyes on Tom: I was going to marry him. I had initially tried to deny my feelings for him, but deep down I knew it. There was such calmness about him. Serenity. That was not anything I was used to, and I loved it. It didn't matter what the "date" was like, or who else was on it with us; I would do anything to spend time with him.

After several months of this ritual, I was running out of movies to get the girls and really tired of eating fried chicken every weekend. Something had to change. I needed more! So I came up with a plan, one that all women should employ if they're trying to bump up their relationship status: every Sunday between services, while Tom was still working at the church, I would go over and clean his house. After all, he was a single man with two little girls and it needed to be done. I gained a huge number of points with this tactic. He appreciated it!

I also let him know he was always on my mind. I went to the store and bought all kinds of different cards, and about every three days I would mail him one. "Just thinking of you," they said. "Glad we are friends." I was relentless.

All my strategies and hard work finally paid off. Walking to his house after Sunday night service one evening, he stopped and put his hands on my shoulders. Turning me so that I faced him, he kissed me. Then he looked into my eyes and said with an enormous amount of sincerity, "I think I love you."

Aaahh! That was the first time in my dating life that a man had told me he loved me *first,* before I blurted it out! I was beyond joyful. The truth was that I loved Tom completely and hearing him say those words made my world feel complete. I had come a long, long way since leaving La-La Land, and life would never be the same.

2

RAINBOWS AHEAD

SUMMER IN AUSTIN WAS fabulous! Fears that my dreams were buried in the sand on a Los Angeles beach were gone, replaced by what can only be described as a giddy, ridiculous discovery: things really didn't stay the same! They could actually get better! Tom and I focused on knowing everything we could about each other, and it was all good. The oppressive heat of a Texas July couldn't knock me off my perch of unadulterated joy. When you're in love, anything seems possible.

Yes, summer was exciting. Then winter started to blow in and I was ready for more. (I'm into change. Call me The Change Agent.) I'm not the kind of person to settle for mediocrity. I needed amplitude in this relationship! I decided I was going to have to sit Tom down and have "the talk." Both men and women know what this is. Women look forward to it because it has the power to move things to a serious place. Men dread it for exactly the same reason. We all know it *must happen*.

I rehearsed my lines for "the talk," and the day came when I delivered them as skillfully as any of the classically trained musicians under Tom's direction. I waited for the reaction that *should* result: "Karen, say no more! I know where you're going with this and I feel *exactly the same way!*" Perhaps a very serious, "I could not agree more. I'm astonished at how much we think alike. I could not be more ready to give my heart to you completely." So what if those responses are straight out of a romance novel? I'm a girl and that's what I wanted to hear.

Instead, Tom tells me he needs time to think. Since he has obviously never read a good romance novel, I give him the benefit of the doubt, remembering that he's a guy. I give him his space. I distract myself with... well, I couldn't distract myself. I had to practically stuff a dishtowel in my mouth to keep from calling him and asking what he was thinking about and why he needed space. What did that mean? Had he not been thinking at all about where we were headed? Did he not *want* to think about it? Why do you need space when you've told someone you're in love with her? Didn't he know that the very next step is to consider where we'll spend the rest of our lives (and now a word from the Goes-Without-Saying Department:) *together*?

It was agonizing, but I waited. I didn't want to blow this by demanding that Tom look at the world exactly as I did. I had already gathered that he wasn't led by his emotions, and as much as I thought emotional leading was perfectly acceptable—no, in fact, the *right* way to lead—I appreciated that he offered a lot of stability to my flights of manic activity. I sweated it out for two full weeks, showing him that I could give him what he'd requested. *You want space? You get space.* Not a word from my mouth. It was hands off.

On a Tuesday night in November the phone rang. It was Tom. "Karen, I've made a decision. I would like to come over and talk." My heart began to pound, but I calmly informed him that I was free and now was as good a time as any. As I hung up the phone, I actually began to pray. This was not something I did frequently, but I had been practicing and was getting better at it.

Tom arrived, all serious and nervous. I didn't know if this was a good sign or a bad sign. I busied myself with asking if he wanted coffee, trying to regulate my pulse under the guise of hospitality.

We settled ourselves on the couch, a tense silence between us. He finally turned to me as though he was preparing to tell me something terrifying. "I'm an alien from the planet Gorgonzola" would not have been as shocking to me as what I feared I might hear—that he didn't want things to go any further, that he wasn't as in love with me as I was with him. "This is it," I think to myself. "Here is the moment of truth. This could be the question I have been waiting to hear or it could be the end-of-my-hopes statement I've been dreading."

Tom spoke quietly. "Karen, I am ready to set a date."

I blinked.

I am ready to set a date? My terror receded but I was acutely aware of how unskilled Tom was in the language of great romance. I knew he could not know that these were not the exact words I was looking for. There were words I needed to hear in order for this to be real. I gently prodded him in the right direction.

"Welllll," I said slowly, "is there something you would like to ask me first?" He looked at me blankly.

I tried again. "There's usually a question that comes first." He thought for a long moment and then said, with all of the finesse of a high school football player who's experienced some serious head injuries, "Yeah. Ummmm." (Slow word search ensues... eyes widen... got it!) "Will you marry me?"

The need to prove I can be calm and composed behind me, I let out a scream. "Of course I will marry you!"

I was ecstatic. This was the best day of my life. I was going to get married! Everything about my wasted time in Los Angeles was gone, wiped away, swept into the warm Pacific Ocean. Everything about my life there was The Past, and now I was looking at My Future. Nothing could touch me! Nothing bad could ever happen again!

As my life filled up with invitations, menus, guest lists, registrations, and every other thing that goes along with a wedding, I pushed all sad things into a mental closet and firmly locked the door. Everything had changed.

As though to confirm my newly righteous place in the universe, I received a letter from one of the many bridal registrations for which I had signed up. I had won Bride of the Month and my prize was a trip to any destination in the world to which Continental Airlines flew and a week's stay at a five-star hotel. Hey—marrying the church guy was really going to pay off! We were already being blessed!

The big day finally arrived: April 17, 1993. It was beautiful. As the doors opened and I stepped into the sanctuary, I caught Tom's eyes and locked onto them as he sang "Household of Faith." Walking down the aisle, my dad at my side, I heard the words as though they were floating into the air toward me: "... When the strong winds blow, it won't fall down. One in Him we'll grow, and the whole world will know that we have a household of faith."

The song was beautiful, but I knew that we would not face strong winds. With our wonderful relationship and love for each other, I did not fear what the lyrics implied. I had already been through enough unhappy experiences to last a lifetime. Now I had a partner with whom to begin the rebuilding process and we were starting with a solid foundation, one built on love and faith. Our fairy tale wedding actually ended with an honest-to-God drive into the sunset. I was going to be happy every day, knowing that my life would be spent with the man I loved.

So we began that life. Tom ran a music business out of our house and I began looking for something I could also do from home. As I pondered what I might pursue, God spoke to my spirit.

This was not a normal occurrence for me; in fact, I barely knew Him. I had a form of relationship with Him, just like a lot of church people who simply have a relationship with *church*. This lulls us into the false security that God is on our side and will bless us if we are good boys and girls. I was head over heels in a fantasy world but the Lord still got through to me, and He began at the most fundamental level with something that let me know He was there: He led me to seek out a new career and soon I started beauty school. I would be a nail professional, the job where you get to talk all day and get paid for it. Sounded like the perfect profession for me, and the Lord gave me the idea for it. I know this sounds silly, but He has to work with what's in front of Him, and at this time in my life it was an indication that He was present.

When I finished school, my little empire opened for business. From Tuesday to Saturday, sun up to sun down, I began to solve nail issues and personal problems citywide. When I had breaks in the "therapy sessions" in the salon, I was able to spend a few moments with my husband. We had become a team. We were both working out of the house during the week and then working together at the church on Sundays, always together and enjoying every spare moment that we could. I'm not kidding: it was bliss. The only fly in the ointment was that every weekend, when we were blessed with Tom's daughters coming to stay with us, I was reminded that I lacked motherly skills. It was hard to jump into being a mom. I became convinced it had to be easier if one started when the child was born. If I did anything right in parenting the Little Angels I was enormously proud of myself; when I did something wrong it would bother me for days. I prayed that God would give me guidance with this new role I had to play. You see, He'd given me direction in my work, so surely I could seek His help with this issue. He was faithful. Slowly I became better at parenting. Sort of.

With this vast experience I had had in hearing God's voice, I was startled by what kept coming up in my head: "India. India. India." That's all I heard. Every time I got quiet, which wasn't often, "India" would rise up inside. I was confused. "What in the world is this about? Am I supposed to go to India? Am I supposed to help someone from India? Wasn't India the name of a character in *Gone With the Wind*? What did *Gone With the Wind* have to do with anything in my life?"

Sure, our church was sponsoring a missions trip in the fall to celebrate the 150th anniversary of William

Carey taking Christianity to India, but I had not even considered going. "India? It's hot there and I love air conditioning. And I just got married!" Why would God tell me this?

I finally told Tom and we decided to pray about what to do. Funny—we got it in our heads that we were supposed to go on this mission trip. It seemed absolutely impossible! Here we were, thinking we needed to get on a plane and fly halfway around the world to this place we had never thought about. But over the next few months, God made a way. People offered to sponsor us. We explained our desire to our clients and they were not inconvenienced by the time we would be away. Things fell into place.

Six weeks before we were scheduled to leave, we began the immunization process required to travel to a third world country. Somewhere between the shots and deep in the preparations for travel, I become aware that something was... well, late. After a week of "I may have just counted wrong," I decided to do what all responsible women do: I went to the drugstore to purchase an EPT test.

When I took the test it showed just a tiny bit of pink. Hmmm. I called the drug store and the pharmacist told me it was a faulty test and I could come back for a new one. I did and got the same result. Had the store received a bad lot? I told Tom, who said calmly, "I know what it is. You're pregnant."

Ridiculous! Too bad he would be proven wrong.

I had to make it through the longest weekend of my life before I could get any answers about the pregnancy test. Two days and three church services and all I could think of were small traces of pink. When a woman believes she may be pregnant, she usually calls the doctor first. Not me; I called EPT. (*They should not manufacture faulty products!*) I was on the phone on Monday at eight in the morning, ready to solve this bizarre mystery.

I explained my pinkish results to the woman on the line and asked why I couldn't get a definite reading. She said the strangest thing: "Ma'am, if there is *any* pink, you have a positive reading."

I hung up on her and then sat motionless, letting reality sink in. "The EPT lady is right. My husband is right. The test is right. I am the only one who is wrong."

This is not to say we were not thrilled! My being pregnant was not unwelcome news; it was only unexpected, coming as it did in the middle of planning an international missions trip. We went to my parents immediately and shared the news. My mother squealed with delight and, after hugs all around, said, "This means you won't be going to India, right?"

I explained that we *would* be going. I figured He knew I would be pregnant and I trusted Him, what little I really knew of Him, to keep me safe. Nothing my mother said could dissuade me; we were moving forward on India.

Since I was "with child," there was a change in my schedule of shots. My doctor said that I could not continue with my immunizations, and because I would not complete them, what I had already obtained would not be effective. I was OK with that. Small sacrifice to make, I decided. I'm German; we don't get sick. Who needs all those shots, anyway?

The day finally came for us to make the twenty-three hour flight to Bangalore, India. When we arrived at the airport it was nighttime, and everything looked normal. As we walked downstairs to baggage claim, however, I realized that things were much different here. The building resembled a concrete warehouse. There was one luggage carousel in the middle. Soldiers were stationed across the room, sitting in folding chairs, holding machine guns. This was not the welcoming committee a pregnant missions worker was hoping for. Nevertheless, we made it to the housing we had been provided and tried to rest for the full days ahead of us.

The day after arrival I was exhausted. More than that, I was starving. Being in India I did not think I would find anything I liked to eat. To my great surprise, the hotel restaurant had the perfect club sandwich. Unfortunately the vegetables on the sandwich had not been cleaned with purified water. Tap water had been used to wash the vegetables I ate. Need I say more?

That night, convinced that someone had dropped a

chainsaw in my body, I had to keep reminding myself that this slight tummy ache would pass. Just an upset stomach; how long could it last?

The next morning I had full-blown salmonella. I found comfort in some of the fellow "victims" who came with us from the United States who had the same "sour stomach" as I.

We had a wonderful team of doctors with us. They went around giving shots to all those who had been stricken, and in half a day, they were as good as new. *They* were, not me. Being pregnant, I had to go with a different kind of remedy. The doctor gave me a Pepto Bismol tablet and offered a smile that reassured me I would be miserable for some time. There was no medicine dispensed for the pregnant woman; just a hurry-up-and-wait expectation for it to take its course.

Seventeen days in India; sixteen and a half of them with an uneasy stomach. Morning sickness really did not look so bad after that.

Despite my stomach issues, God actually used the team. We went from town to town teaching how to have Sunday school and vacation Bible school. Then we would evangelize in the slums and baptize wherever we could. It was amazing to see the kingdom of God and the Word being spread throughout a nation, right before my eyes. It started a change in me. I was witnessing the Lord in action. If for no other reason, I was supposed to go to

India to see how God can move. It's a wonder He didn't see a way to do that in my hometown on my native soil, but that's how God is sometimes. He'll take you halfway around the world to show you the simplest, most beautiful truth about Himself.

This doesn't mean I was new inside, with a hunger to experience who God was and what He had for me. I was basking in an experience that cracked the door to my soul open. It was something different than I had experienced before. I had never seen myself as someone who would go on a missions trip. This experience made me feel I was worthy to be a church worker. Truly having an understanding of God's grace and a desire to give my life to Him completely was not on my radar yet. But this was a start, and on the flight home, I felt honored to have been a part of something so special.

For the remainder of months before I was due, I was like a sunflower in full bloom. I had the perfect job in which to be pregnant; clients brought me snacks on the hour. After all, it's dangerous to go without nutrition during pregnancy. I loved it! Topping it off was the constant emotion of carrying a precious little gift from God inside of me. I embraced every moment and tried to put all that I was feeling into my mental database. I wanted to hold the moments forever.

The pregnancy was long, as is any pregnancy during summertime in Texas, but there were no complications.

No worries. Before we knew it the day came for me to be induced. A week late in delivering, I was very ready to get rid of a few pounds, but they didn't come off easily. There was the whole pushing thing and by golly, there was some serious difficulty, but that little bundle of joy made his way into the world on July 8, 1994. James Allen Mayer was my very healthy, nine-pound, six-ounce boy, which my doctor announced by saying, "He weighs more than a gallon of milk." I had been doing that pushing exercise and was rather exhausted, so all I could muster was a puzzled squint in his direction. He explained, "A gallon of milk is only eight pounds." (What a comedian! What priceless trivia! I wondered if he would put it on the birth certificate.)

My little James was perfect. Unable to understand what I had done in my life to deserve such a blessing, I thanked God endlessly. Tom and I were so happy, so blessed that God had entrusted us with this beautiful child. The sense of responsibility is immediate!

So was the love. I had no idea you could love something so much, so quickly. There was an instant connection. A hole I never realized I had got filled in the instant James was placed in my arms. I had heard this love discussed among parents but I had never known it for myself. I finally understood.

We went home from the hospital and although I was the mother, it turned out that Tom had more of the maternal instinct. He showed me how to change diapers and care for the baby. I watched the father-son bond form right in front of me, observing how Tom talked to James, cooed at him, held him.

We were model parents. We missed nothing. We took in every moment watching him grow and develop into a smart, wonderful toddler. He was advanced for his age in everything he did. (I am sure every mom believes this to be true of her child, but my James was the real deal.)

I did my share of compare-and-compete with other moms. "When was your child rolling over? Crawling? Pulling up?" Just to make sure James was above the curve, I had to ask these questions. I discovered I was not the only one; this is apparently a "mommy" thing. Mommies must probe other mothers about milestones in our kids' lives. Instead of just letting our babies be babies, we push them to grow up, and we want them to do it at the same time or (preferably) before everyone else their age.

Fortunately for me, and for my competitive nature, James did. The first year and a half of his life flew by while he absorbed the world around him each and every day.

3
TORNADO WATCH

MONTHS PASSED, OUR CHILD grew, and each new thing he learned to do made us so excited. Each new discovery was a cause for clapping and celebrating. Never-ending cheerleading made our days happy and full of life. We were blessed, blessed, blessed! Our little baby James was growing up into a smart and handsome little being with such a unique personality and happiness that spread to everyone who came near him.

But at eighteen months, something happened. The learning came to a halt. Being above the curve stopped. James was suddenly different. Something inside of him was different. It started with the head banging.

One day, James ran down the hallway and hit his head right into the wall. I thought what any mother would: "What a boy!" I thought he had just lost control in his enthusiasm, playing rough like little men do. I made sure he was OK and sent him on his way.

But he did it again, and then again, intentionally. He ran to throw himself at the same spot in the wall, over and over. Tom and I were dumbfounded. He had never acted this way before. We held him, spoke quietly to him, thinking maybe he was just having some kind of emotional episode. We told him everything was going to be all right. He calmed down. We kissed him and set him on his feet.

He ran straight for the wall. He sat with his back to it and began pounding his head hard, as though it gave him some kind of relief.

Not having been a mother before, I had no idea if this was some kind of boy behavior I did not understand. In desperation, I planted him in front of the television set, hoping to distract him from this frightening compulsion. He fixed his eyes on the screen as though a personal message was being sent to his brain. "Well, OK," I thought. "That's different, but at least he's not head banging." Perhaps he was just reaching an age where the TV was going to hold a special fascination for him.

I had a sense that something was wrong but like so many clueless parents, I didn't want to overreact. I decided I would keep an eye on things to see how they played out. James had recently begun coming into our room at night to crawl into bed with us, and we welcomed his warm, sleepy little body. "He's just having growing pains," I told myself. "He's adjusting. This is simply an adjustment phase of some kind."

But the head banging became a daily occurrence, and

sitting him in front of the television set was the only way I could curtail it. I would pop in a video and press "play" and check his head for bruises. The television was a pacifier, but in a far more powerful way than most parents think of it. He seemed to need it, to draw something from it. I purchased loads of videos and tried to rationalize the situation as simply something my unique son required at this time.

Tom and I were doing well enough in our businesses at this point—he was teaching music from home and I had opened a salon—that we had moved into a very nice house in a very upscale neighborhood and had the money to hire a gifted live-in domestic. Marta adored James and was able to work with him. Hispanic women seem to have such a love for children, and I think they especially dote upon little boys. She called him "Baby Yames" and slept in his room each night. This was exceedingly helpful, because his odd behavior was becoming more than I could manage and I wondered if I had really been fooling myself about my ability to be any kind of good mother.

Marta was the best thing that ever happened to me. Maybe it was a combination of her being twice my age and the fact that she was a grandmother that made her so calm and accepting of everything. "It's OK!" she'd say when James began to flip out. He seemed to sense her extreme nurturing hardwiring and responded to her with adoration. She took care of things. From Sunday night to Friday night, I trusted in Marta.

I escaped to work. By this time, I had a dedicated clientele of women, most of whom who were older than me. They would regale my staff and me (and each other) with the typical can-you-top-this stories of childbirth and child rearing that are the stuff of female legend. "Ralphie jumped off the garage roof fourteen times in three weeks when he was nine, and I don't know how he got off with just a broken ankle," one might say. "That's nothing," an elderly bronzed-and-beautified woman with a smoker's voice might kick back. "My Harold took our truck and drove to Houston and back in the middle of the night with the family dog every week for six months before we figured out why we were wasting so much money on gas. We finally caught him when he knocked over the trashcan pulling into the driveway after one of his nighttime trips. He was only eleven!"

I'm exaggerating, but you get the picture. These were strong Texas women who had raised cattle and reared children and managed husbands and kept their families afloat. They were wealthy, well groomed, and tough. They'd survived drug abuse (theirs and others), philandering men, low-life in-laws, bankruptcy, domestic abuse, criminal offspring, and more. These women were my only real role models. They didn't seem to think there was anything wrong with James.

As I told them bits and pieces of what was going on with my son, I got as many different answers as I had clients:

"You're not disciplining him enough."

"You're disciplining him too much."

"You're not spending enough time with him."

"James is spoiled."

"My son did the same thing! Don't worry about it."

"He's in the terrible twos. It will pass."

But it didn't pass. Hitting his head on the wall was just the beginning. He would stand in front of that television set for hours without talking; just staring. I am talking *hours*. If we turned the television off, he began throwing a tantrum that was stunning in its intensity. We would turn the television back on to placate him. Sometimes while gazing zombie-like at the television, without any warning at all he would run up to the set and attempt to push it over.

It moved on to a fascination with rubber. We would find James chewing on erasers. We didn't know what to make of this. I really thought it might be just a kid thing. Kids chew on stuff, right? Is it really that abnormal that my child is chewing the erasers from every pencil in the house?

But it was not just rubber erasers. Maybe we would have found a way to handle erasers, but we couldn't hold back the shock that began to settle in our chests where our hearts were pounding with disbelief as the extent of James's rubber obsession unfolded. We began to find teeth marks in the backs of our bathroom rugs and pieces of rubber missing from them. Then we noticed that he had been eating the rubber lining on our car doors; he was not just chewing, he was *eating*. These pieces of rubber were gone, ingested into his system. He swallowed the whole mess.

This bizarre behavior went on for months. It got worse gradually, a little each day, and maybe that's why I didn't take action. Sometimes things happen and you look on and think to yourself, "Did I just see that? Did that really happen?" You rationalize behavior, especially in a child, and the enormity of the changes doesn't quite sink in. But when James was two, I saw something that nearly knocked me out. I walked into the kitchen just as he had managed to move a chair over to the sink. He reached in and grabbed the rubber stopper and he was eating it. Like a dog with a bone. Like an animal.

All I could think was, "God, please let this be a phase. Please let him grow out of this." But I knew. Deep down in my gut I knew it was not a phase. I knew there was something horribly wrong with my child.

Still, I did not seek medical attention, even while realizing that it was getting worse. Hitting his head on the wall was not enough; he began to actually *slam* his head through the wall and then eat the drywall from the hole he made. Consoling him was not an option. He would scream, throwing a fit that had no entrance and no exit. He was trapped inside some terrible place that provided no escape. Communication was slowly ceasing. Tom and I were shut out.

If we went to the park for an afternoon to play on the swings, James would find a bicycle and try to eat one of the tires. We would chat with someone wearing flip-flops, who would suddenly discover James trying to eat the shoes right off her feet. I was becoming very sure there was no way this was just a phase. I was too frightened to want to know what might be the problem. I simply shut it out, justifying his weird behavior in any way I could. My child could not be sick. He could not be defective. It could not be possible.

As time went on, his appetite became as limited as his ability to communicate with us. Rubber appealed to him but real food did not. For a boy who would eat anything when he was a baby, the habits he was developing now were stupefying. The only things he would eat were eggs, milk, cheese, sausage, and Cheetos. The combination was not conducive to his health, and his digestive system was terribly messed up.

I knew this was not right. Things were *not right*! But some of us, when we live with something every single day, make ourselves used to it, especially if we're secretly terrified. We don't always realize how bad it is and, day after day, we fall into a kind of routine of weirdness that seems manageable. If we don't have a clue what to do, we just keep struggling to maintain.

I was exhausted and afraid. I lived with fear every day: fear that my child was psychotic; fear that things would never change; fear that his next bizarre behavior would be too much for me to handle because, believe it or not, I was handling my son's antics. I look back in complete wonder that Tom and I did manage each day. Did we tell ourselves this was normal? No. But we rationalized: who really had a "normal" life? Maybe this was simply the hand we were dealt. People handle far worse. For me, avoidance and denial were coping mechanisms. I was fearful down to my bones; I was filled with anxiety, sleep deprived, and isolated. I knew something was too wrong to ignore—but I ignored and managed and coped.

While I gave limited information to my role-model clients who fed me somewhat reassuring stories of their adventures with wild youngsters, Tom never told his music students anything. If James was throwing a fit somewhere in the house that could be heard in his office, Tom simply ignored it. When James exhibited his increasingly outrageous behaviors, he made no mention of it, nor did his students. No one felt comfortable saying anything. It was all so strange. What do you say to your music teacher when you catch his son trying to eat the rubber lining on the trunk of your mother's car when you're stowing your instrument after a lesson? You politely ignore it and wonder what in the world is wrong with that kid.

We were deeply ashamed. I tried to talk with Tom about getting some kind of help for James. He didn't encourage me, and he didn't deny me. Tom wasn't going to fight. His way of dealing with this awful situation was to say, "Everything's going to work itself out." These words were his panacea for anything and everything, no matter how urgent. For instance, his mother, a woman to whom he was deeply devoted, battled breast cancer and underwent a mastectomy. When I urged him to get together with his brothers to find out what kind of prognosis she had received, he responded, "If it's really bad, she'll tell us." I pointed out that having a mastectomy was an indication that something might be really bad. He shook it off. "If it was really that bad, someone would tell us that something's wrong." He and his brothers would not confront the issue, and she would not bring it up. She died of her disease, and her sons were devastated by the "unexpected" loss.

While I found this approach to life extremely puzzling, I viewed Tom as a spiritual giant. He knew the Bible. He could quote Scripture, and he always knew what to say in that church-lingo responsive way: "God doesn't give us more than we can bear," and "All things work together for good." In my heart, I wondered about that. This was shaping up to be more than I could bear, and I didn't see any good in what was happening to our child. My husband didn't seem to find it necessary to find out if there was something wrong with James. It might say something about *him*, and that would definitely have been too much to bear.

But it's what Tom said about me that cut so deeply. "If you were a good mother," he told me, "this wouldn't be happening." He was a music teacher; I was a gossipy salon owner who talked all day long. What I was doing had no value, and it was probably why James was acting out. I felt deeply hurt and angry. Maybe he was right, but my successful business was aiding our fine lifestyle and helping to pay for our live-in help. We could not live as we did on his teaching wages alone.

Where in the world had my fairy tale romance gone? How could I have known that less than three years into my marriage, my husband, the spiritual giant, would be flogging me with guilt? Secretly, I believed I deserved it. I knew he must be right. This was all my fault. My past was catching up with me. God had allowed me a brief moment of happiness, and now He was letting me know what He really thought of me. I guess those strong winds Tom sang about at our wedding had finally arrived. Time for a part of my heart to get to the cellar with Auntie Em. The rest of me was swept up into the twister.

4
POSSIBLE FLOODING

I FINALLY GATHERED MY COURAGE and took James to the pediatrician. I told him of the insanity I saw in my child. I didn't use the word *insane*, of course. That was my deepest terror, but I was not going to give it a voice. I just recounted every bizarre activity with increasing hysteria, sure that the doctor was going to have James carted away to a pediatric mental ward somewhere. He was not moved by this emotional mother. He wasn't moved by the clearly disturbed child, either. He examined James, made his notes, and later called to tell me there was nothing out of the ordinary with the blood work he'd ordered. He gave James a diagnosis of PDD-NOS, Pervasive Developmental Disorder, Not Otherwise Specified. I selectively heard the "nothing out of the ordinary" as the assessment and ran with it.

I was so relieved I cried. There was nothing wrong with James! Nothing wrong! Blood values normal! Pervasive Developmental Disorder didn't sound so terrible. He was disordered developmentally, but not broken. How I filed these things away so I would not have to face them is something I look back on with amazement.

So what was the problem? Was I just overreacting to some unique childhood manifestations I had never heard of? Was he going to grow out of them? Was my clientele right about what they viewed as typical crazy kid stuff?

I was so confused I couldn't think. So I didn't. I pushed it all aside, thanked my lucky stars for precious Marta, who dealt with my little boy with miraculous affection, and tuned out everything my husband told me except for one thing: everything was going to work itself out.

Things seemed manageable enough for me to become pregnant again. I don't know why I thought things seemed manageable, but they did. Our respective businesses were thriving. I had received some further training in my field and had begun traveling to trade shows all over the country as an instructor. Marta had James under a semblance of control; his behavior was not better, but it was being maintained. We kept a stack of videos rewound and ready to pop in the machine whenever he was found eating rubber or drywall. It had gotten to the point that if there was no picture on the television, James would shriek and become hysterical until the "play" button was pushed and the screen lit up with an image. Even rewinding was an unpleasant experience. Once there was a picture, he would immediately become quiet and transfixed. Whoever was watching him simply had to remember to keep an eye on his penchant for suddenly rushing to the set to push it over.

He had to have that television on all the time. He had started to get up very early, even if he was sleeping with Tom and me, and we would get him settled in front of the TV in what was essentially the middle of the night. He was sleeping only about four hours, no matter what time he went to bed.

We got a television for his room, and we would be awakened at all hours to the raised volume of whatever he was watching. I couldn't understand why he wasn't asleep on his feet; I certainly was. This did give us an excuse for James's behavior when we were out with him, however; we could always say, "He's tired." No matter what strange or awful thing he did, it could be blamed on his being tired. Being away on my professional trips was a relief. They gave Tom more reason, though, to remind me further of what a rotten mother I was.

So in my twisted emotional state, I decided having another child would be a good thing. When nothing is normal, irrational decisions don't seem at all irrational. I convinced myself a baby would be good for the family. When James was two and a half years old, we were blessed with a baby girl. On November 1, 1996, Paige Allison arrived, perfect, beautiful, just as James had been.

I felt like we had a new start. "James just needs something to do," I thought absurdly. "Someone to play and talk with. A sister to distract him from doing the things he's doing." Paige was the answer. She was going to make things better for us, for all of us—especially James.

I had to believe this. I had to believe that Paige was the answer to my prayers, because if she was not, if I did not truly believe this, I would have to face the sickening truth that life was never going to change. Life would never get better. My son would always be this out of control *thing* forever. I was not ready to embrace or accept that. No! Things were changing. I just knew it.

Reality started to hit hard with Paige's birth. I did not know what I had been thinking when I decided to have another child. I had been in a state of delusion. Now I had an infant in addition to a toddler I could not control. I cannot tell you why I thought this would add up to the perfect solution. I started to allow the thought that something was seriously, terribly wrong with James. Maybe he was so different from other kids that we needed outside intervention. It was exceptionally difficult for me to admit this even though James was growing worse as the days progressed.

When I brought Paige home it seemed to set James off even more. She did not demand a lot of attention. She was a perfect baby. Perfect! (Wait—I think I have said this before.) She did need attention, though; she actually required feeding, changing, and interaction. She needed some attention, and James did not like this.

Before Paige, it was all about James; he got all of our attention and time. He had time to negotiate, manipulate, and trick us, which was how we viewed his actions. We saw James as doing whatever he needed to do to get what he wanted. His tantrums were not cries for help or indications of impairment. They were, we thought, strictly demands for our attention. Now his time was being interrupted, taken from him and given to Paige. He was already always angry, and not just plain old angry, but filled with rage.

The first day we brought Paige home, James ate the rubber handle off of her infant carrier. I felt like the earth should just open up and swallow me whole. I knew it was a signal that Paige was not welcome, and I was sick inside, not to mention that constant in-my-face truth that my son ate rubber on a daily basis. I had to keep him separated from her. We got rid of everything that had any rubber in it, but what a surprise, huge numbers of products for newborns are made of rubber: pacifiers, toys, teethers—everything! It was a terrific challenge.

Tom and I, knowing what he could do to drywall and bicycle tires, began to fear what he might be capable of doing to Paige. We were terrified. It made me nervous all day and kept me awake all night.

Then the unthinkable occurred: Marta gave me her

notice. She could not juggle managing James and caring for a newborn at the same time. How could she? Tom and I couldn't even do one of those things, and here was an angel from heaven who had kept our son from descending deep into animalistic behavior. Now she was leaving us, and I was devastated.

For a while, I listened to the advice of some of my clients that his antics were the result of not having enough discipline. Maybe James needed more structure in the house. Because we had live-in help who assisted us, the thought of school had not entered the picture, but even the kids I knew who were in school were not behaving like this. They were disciplined.

This line of thinking got me through a couple of months. I tried more discipline, but it did not work. When James wanted something he would turn red and *implode*. As soon as this happened he would get whatever he wanted, because it made life easier to give in to the tantrums. I knew I was not exerting proper procedures, but at this point I was just trying to survive. I was trying to find some way to comfort myself with the fact that I had to get through another hour, another day, another year—a lifetime of this misery. Hope was fading. My world grew darker. With two to take care of, it started to seem impossible.

I was blessed during this time, though, with another precious live-in named Camellia. She started in January with tons of energy, quite young but acting as though she knew exactly what to do. She thought James was simply going through the terrible twos and she worked indulgently with him. She was great with Paige, too, and her youth and vitality lightened our load.

Early in 1997, a tiny ray of light entered my life when one of my clients, a teacher, informed me that in the state of Texas, if a child is speech delayed he or she can start school at three years old. James was going to be three in the summer. "Maybe *that's* it," I thought. "Speech delayed." I could handle this idea. It didn't sound bad or frightening. You see, I couldn't allow explanations that might be bad news for me. My philosophy was that if I didn't hear bad news, I could work around things. Denial is a powerful force. I liked the possibility that this might be a way to get some help for James that didn't sound too extreme.

I told Tom about the program, and we gathered the information. Tom took James in for what was referred to as an "intake," which made me nervous. It sounded mental hospital-like. I asked Tom to take James to the intake appointment. In spite of Tom's avoidance in facing our issues, he was better with James than I was. He was patient and kind, and could handle the tantrums in a way I simply could not. He always seemed to know what to do and his personality was the type that just didn't get worked up about things.

The truth was, I didn't think I could stand for outsiders to observe my little boy like he was a science experiment and then have them tell me there was something wrong. I knew, somewhere inside, that this would be the diagnosis; I just didn't want to hear it. Tom was the designated parent for the intake, and I waited for the assessment.

After the evaluation, it was decided that he qualified for the program. You would think I would be thrilled, but my spirits plummeted. You see, I had known they were going to tell us he needed help, but once he was accepted into the program, I had to acknowledge that I had a child who needed help from the state of Texas. It was shattering. I added the blow to my load of depression-inducing factors that I carried around in an enormous sack of pain deep within, stuffed it into a closet in my mind, and pushed forward.

There was one thing I could get excited about: the elementary school he was to attend was across the street from our house! In spite of my denial, I tried to be positive, but I was nervous about the meeting scheduled with the school administrators. Meeting with the principal was never a good thing when I was in school. I was sure that had not changed. But the principal and the members of the teaching team were very supportive and encouraging and it was obvious they wanted to put me at ease. They went over schedules, classroom guidelines, and everything else we needed to know about the program.

They explained that James would be in a classroom with other children and that their focus would be on modifying his behavior.

I asked if James would be kicked out of the program if he threw a fit. They all looked at me with puzzled expressions and finally one of them answered, "Of course not. He's a Special Education student." I blinked. "Special Education"? My James?

The baby who had been born perfect and healthy was "Special Ed"? I fought back tears. This was not what I had thought I was signing up for when my precious little boy was placed into my arms for the first time. I had planned on a model childhood, brilliant development milestones, and indications that he was above average. "Special Ed" was never on my radar of possible scenarios for my son. I cannot explain the despair I felt. I arose each morning with a sick dread, working to pull myself together.

I could not give in to that despair, though, and survive mentally, so I focused on the good. "This is a great thing for James," I reminded myself. "These people are going to give him rules, and they are going to help him catch up. He's just a little behind, but soon he will be right where he is supposed to be." I purchased fresh, new school supplies for him, and decided this was a new start. Soon this nightmare would be behind us, and we wouldn't ever hear the words "Special Needs" or "Special Education" again.

5
HURRICANE SEASON

I T IS FUNNY HOW time can seem to go fast and slow all in the same period. I could hardly believe James was already going to start his first year of school. While I may have felt a little happy about it, it didn't alter the goings-on at home. Each day dragged on more painful than the last. The wild behaviors James exhibited did not let up just because he was about to enter a Special Education program, and I didn't get it. Wasn't this supposed to be the answer to my problems? So why hadn't things changed?

The first day of school arrived. Most parents are excited for their children on the first day of school, remembering to pack a lunch and find out what time to arrive to pick the child up at the end of the day. I was too focused on trying to remember the name of the program my child was entering. My James did not just start school, you see; he got to start a Special Education program called "Preparing Preschoolers in Child Development." Doesn't that sound weightier than simply "going to school"? I wasn't 100 percent sure of the purpose of the program, to be honest. It had been hard enough to hear he needed it, and I hadn't listened much beyond that. What I did know was the school system was going to help. These folks were going to fix James. He wasn't broken; he just needed a little maintenance.

After a while, I did see changes, or maybe it was what I wanted to see. In any event, each day he returned to the house with homework and activities to complete. The program obviously gave parents and children a direction on which to focus. We could move toward the same goal: helping James.

Tom and I desperately needed focus. In addition to our respective careers, we were interim music directors, filling in at churches that didn't have one. Our normal schedule was two services on Sunday morning, one service on Sunday night, and one again on Wednesday night, sent to a different church every three or four months. This schedule was wearing, and it meant leaving James in a different nursery each time, with new workers who did not understand his issues. Of course, I was in such a fantasy blindness about his issues that I probably never explained them well to the unwitting nursery staffs, so when they were hit full force with his conduct it must have been a stunner. Few church nursery workers are trained in special needs, and even if they are able to handle a special needs child it is usually one that requires little more than being watchful for an hour or two.

It became almost unbearable for me to give the same speech three or four times a week to the clueless nursery worker of the day, often just a teenager. "My son, James, has some very different behaviors from the other kids you take care of. He's going to eat rubber, hit himself in the head, and probably vomit at least once. Other than that, though, he's fine!" (How would *you* respond upon hearing something like that? *Exactly.*) I never knew what to expect when I picked him up at the end of a service. I faced women young and old whose eyes were big with fear and loathing as they returned my child to me. Some of them could not speak. I was becoming tired of defending and explaining my child's actions when I didn't under-stand them myself. It was unfair to ask church workers to accept what even I could not.

There were stares. Not looks of sympathy or empathy; not the general glances of annoyance from non-parents who judge you worthless at rearing children. It was sheer disgust and revulsion I saw on people's faces. Bit by bit, my denial bubble was beginning to crack. I started to feel the war zone in which I lived. Things were always in chaos, and what I had convinced myself was normal was clearly reflected in the faces of people around me as not normal. I saw my son through the eyes of others, observing his rage and his psychotic tantrums. I would have stared in contempt, too, at such outrageous displays from others, had my son been the perfect little boy I had expected. But here I was, living in my upended version of normal, and it pained me to watch people making severe judgments about it.

I asked myself if I could do the interim church music thing anymore. I didn't know if I had it in me to keep explaining the special care required, or encounter one more nursery worker who looked like she'd been to hell and back, or catch one more stranger staring at us out of my peripheral vision... staring at James.

The hardest questions of all were on a constant loop in my head, day in and day out: Where is God? Why isn't He coming to help us? We're doing His work. We're employed in His kingdom! For goodness' sake, I had been to India as a missions worker! Didn't I deserve a little assistance for that? But I couldn't ignore what Tom seemed rather fond of pointing out: I was a bad mother. This was my fault. We were being punished because of my sins, my inadequacies, my bad choices, and sordid past. It figured. I was already so low, this just made sense, and it gave me more reason to want to check out of the church scene altogether.

As I struggled with the absence of answers, I found some comfort in the progress James seemed to be making at school. I really did see improvement in just a few months. His teacher would send notes home to keep Tom and me updated on daily activities, and we would send notes back that told her of what transpired after school and weekends. If there was something to feel good about, it was this—partnership with professionals.

Nevertheless, I continued to throw myself into work so that I could escape my daily agony. I have always been a hard worker, but I had become a workaholic. It was simply less painful to work like crazy than to accept the entire less-than-perfect child situation. It was hard to look at him sometimes, especially with all his difficulties in functioning. It was hard to be around him. I admit there were times when it was hard to like him.

He started to wander out of the house. Not at night, but during the day he would fiddle with doorknobs, and he figured out how to undo the lock and open the front door. People would discover this big kid in diapers from that house down the street ringing doorbells and running off. It might have been cute once, but after a while our neighbors just didn't like us. There would be a knock on the front door and we would find one of them with James in tow and an exasperated look on their faces, telling us, "I found your son again." We would politely thank them and take James in. Our behavior must have looked odd; after all, what four-year-old still wears a diaper? They couldn't know that James could not be potty trained. We weren't rocked by his antics anymore. We just decided he would stay at home except for school. We went nowhere with him. Tom and I took turns staying at home. If there was no one to take care of James, we did not go anywhere together.

We lost Camellia to a job where she could earn more money. I scrambled to find someone else because there was no way I could give up the only thing that was keeping me halfway sane—my business—and stay home with a child I could barely tolerate. I found Rosario. To my astonishment, she was able to deal with the extremes of James's activities and the daily routine of child care for Paige, just as Camellia had been doing. Although I was relieved and felt supremely blessed, I wondered if this said something about me. Three other women were able to artfully handle my boy. Why couldn't I? What was wrong with me? Was Tom correct? Was I a bad mother? My guilt was crushing. I retreated further into my work.

One Thursday afternoon I could not trade escape for reality. I answered my phone at work to hear Tom's voice. "Karen." I knew instantly something was wrong.

"Karen, I am not kidding," he said, with a shut-down-everything very serious voice. "There is a woman at our door from Child Protective Services. She just came from the elementary school where she had James take all of his clothes off so she could check him for bruises."

What? Child Protective Services (CPS)? Clothes off? Bruises? While I was trying to process what I had just heard, he went on. "She wants to ask you some questions.

There has been a report filed of harm or neglect to James. Hold on—here she is."

The woman introduced herself and asked if now was a good time or did I want a moment to gather my thoughts. I began to spit out an answer, and then realized it was probably not the time to be clever. "No," I responded, trying to sound calm and in control. "Now is fine."

Like bullets out of a gun, she began a battery of questions.

"Do you have sex in front of your child?"

"No."

"Do you have the Playboy channel?"

"No."

"Do you think it is normal that your son sits and rocks and puts his head through the drywall?"

"No."

"Do you think it is normal that he doesn't speak at this age, still takes a bottle, and eats only about three or four foods?"

"No."

Anger ignited inside like a match on gasoline. What part of "no" might be confusing to her? Could the inappropriateness of firing questions at me on the phone be a procedure she's actually required to follow? With every last bit of strength I had, I kept my mouth shut, a bona fide miracle. There are some situations in which it is very simply in one's best interests to answer briefly and add nothing.

Finally, she said, "Your answers match up with your husband's. I must inform you that you are under investigation by the state. I will leave a pamphlet that tells you where to bring your attorney if we take your son into custody."

My heart was pounding so hard I was sure I would pass out. Just when I thought life could not get worse, she added: "Oh, and one more thing. Within the next 48 hours you need to take James to your pediatrician and have him checked for anal tears and enlarged genitals."

I am sure the conversation took only a few minutes, but it felt like it lasted an hour. I drove home in a fog. I had a child I couldn't control. I couldn't get him to speak, and I had no clue how to alter his behavior. I was fully aware of how much I wanted to avoid embracing the hand I had been dealt, but this I could not avoid. We were being investigated because someone thought we were abusing him, perhaps sexually.

I once read about a man whose arm got caught in a huge shredder. He told a reporter that he could feel his arm being stretched, felt the flesh in his armpit beginning to tear. As he screamed for help and a coworker hit the emergency stop, he knew the arteries and nerves had been pulled from his shoulder. That describes a little of how I felt: my arms were being pulled from my body because some burdens were proving too heavy to carry. The weight was just too much. Taking a breath was so difficult I wondered if my ribs were broken. How much can a human being really take?

I walked into the house and into Tom's arms, and we stood and wept together, both of us just as damaged from what we were going through as our son was. James had no way to tell us what was happening to him. We had no one to whom we could release our fears and emotions— not even each other. Our dysfunction as a couple was not to feel, not to ask questions, not to address the issues. But now, somehow, some way, in spite of our enormous personal impairments, we had to gather ourselves and take the next logical step.

As soon as I could speak, I called the school to find out what was going on. James was pretty much only at school or at home so I assumed someone from the school had called CPS. To my astonishment, the principal said, "You know, sometimes these things happen."

"Sometimes these things happen." That didn't sound like a response worthy of the gravity of the moment, and it wasn't good enough for me. In fact, I could feel myself break out in a sweat and detected a sharp increase in my blood pressure. I walked across the street to the school, freely expressing the change in outlook I had experienced since the morning's momentous phone call. (Translation:

I was sobbing and nearly hysterical.) I went to James's room and walked into a chamber vibrating with critical disapproval. His teacher and the aides looked at me like I was the abuser and pedophile someone had claimed I was. By the time James and I made it to the principal's office, I was a wreck, but I wanted to get to the bottom of this. I wanted to fix it.

The principal actually calmed me down. He told me he was sure the report had been made by someone unfamiliar with special needs children. He or she saw my child's out-of-the-ordinary behavior and felt it necessary to report it to an outside agency instead of inquiring with the school administration. He urged me to do what CPS instructed and promised that the school would provide a full report attesting to James's enrollment in the state-sponsored special program.

His assurances helped some, but I went home and cried a little more. I was exhausted. In spite of all my dismissive tendencies, I actually was doing every single thing I knew to do. It wasn't like I was sitting back, flat-out pretending nothing was wrong. I was flying blind in getting help for my son, and God knows I wasn't logically evaluating what I really needed to do, but I was doing *something*. I was operating on emotions, a hefty dose of denial, and a mother's desperate love. Now I was faced with an official voice telling me I had dropped the ball in a huge way, and it might mean James would be taken from us. Call me crazy, but while I might have fantasized about James being somewhere else, having him forcefully removed from our home was not part of that picture.

Tom and I actually prayed. I don't remember what made us do that, except we felt it was called for. We should have done that a long time before, but we were stumbling along with the knowledge we had, as dysfunctional spiritually as we were emotionally. We were clueless when it came to facing struggles with real faith and intercession. Tom knew how to quote Scripture. Both of us knew how to sound like we had been around the block. The truth was we had never left the parking lot, but it is easy in the church world to look like you're something you're not. Now we were exposed. Looking back, I praise the Lord that we at least knew it was important that we pray together about our son, no matter how late in the game we got this tremendous revelation.

We prayed that God would work it all out. We prayed the way we had heard others pray. We told ourselves the situation was in His hands. It felt good to do something constructive together, even if I gained little hope from the activity.

The next day I called the doctor's office. When the receptionist asked me the reason for the visit, I could feel myself dying inside with each word I spoke, but this was no time to minimize the situation. "My husband and I are being investigated by Child Protective Services and we need to have James checked for bruises, enlarged genitals, and anal tears. We need to have the doctor document and file his conclusions with the state within the next couple of days."

There was very little sound on the other end of the line other than the noises of appointment book pages being turned and finally, she offered a time for the doctor to see James. I can't begin to imagine what was going through her head.

The doctor saw us. We paid. We left. We waited. We waited for a letter from the doctor. We waited for a visit from CPS. We waited for something that would allow us to breathe once again. But nothing happened.

For months, we heard nothing. My calls to CPS were not returned. Then finally, on Super Bowl Sunday in January of 1998, the telephone rang.

"Is this Mrs. Mayer?" asked a crisp voice on the other end.

"Yes, it is," I replied.

"Mother of James Allen Mayer?"

"Yes." My heart began pounding wildly and I took deep, silent breaths.

"This is Child Protective Services. We wanted to let you know that our investigation regarding James is complete and we have found no wrongdoing. The investigation is closed," she said, and with a "good-bye" she hung up. I didn't even get a chance to ask why I was called on a Sunday, although I was glad they hadn't waited another day.

I hung up the phone and burst into tears. I gave Tom the news, determined to use the wonderful discipline of prayer more often. I turned over a new leaf as a form of thanks.

6
TSUNAMI

I HAVE OPERATED MY WHOLE life with the notion that if there is a problem, you should find the solution and fix it. I was an expert at fixing things for myself and for others (whether they wanted me to or not). All one has to do is learn everything about the problem. To conquer it, you devour it. Of course, one has to admit there is a problem, and I was only sort of willing to do this. I didn't want to admit how serious the problem was. But I felt that I could fix it if I could find a solution.

That's what I was going to do with James. I would find out everything I could about his condition and once I knew what I was dealing with, I would find a way to make it better. "I will find a way to make it right," I said over and over. Because I did not know what I was facing, I didn't know what steps to take, but now I was determined to learn more.

I made up my mind to forgive whoever had reported us. The principal had been right—these things happen, and someone had been looking out for James's welfare, even if they had done it in the clumsiest and most insensitive of ways. But he was OK, and now that we could put the CPS episode behind us, he was going to get better.

Something good actually came of the trauma with CPS—it led us to Star Bright Pediatrics, an agency that would bring greater clarity and honest-to-God *help*. One of the teachers at school mentioned Star Bright when she heard what we were going through, and suggested we take James there. After looking into it, I thought they might at least be able to tell me specifically what was going on with my son. That would be a start.

I decided to go to the assessment meeting. Part of my new leaf-turning decision was to be more proactive, and I felt both Tom and I should go to the appointment. As we got ready, I tried to insert my will into James with those two words most parents use taking their children out: "Act right." Still keeping one toe in the pool of denial, I figured that if he would act right they would tell me he was just having a rough season and was going to outgrow this behaviorally difficult stage. In order to get him to act right, I begged, pleaded, and bribed him, as I had so many times before. I told him if he would act very, very good while we were there, he would get a great surprise when we got done. We had no health insurance at this point (and companies were not lining up to give our unique situation a policy), so we paid cash for everything. Doctor bills were already expensive, so to have to buy toys every time we wanted our child to attempt to behave normally was one of the biggest expenses we had.

We signed in at Star Bright, and soon James and Tom and I were ushered into a small room with little chairs, tables, and toys. A doctor began to observe James and take notes. She would hand him a toy and then ask for it back to see his reaction. I was pleased; he was doing well, handling the "poking and prodding" better than I thought he would.

He picked up a toy airplane and was examining it when the doctor abruptly took it from him. James began to throw a fit. I tried to smile, thinking it would help me control my dread. He went into one of his full-blown, over-the-top fits. He threw himself down on the floor, scooted up against the wall and slammed his head back and forth. Then the screaming started, louder than normal. This fit was worse than I had seen in some time. I wished the floor would open up and swallow me.

The doctor began to write feverishly, completely ignoring what was going on in front of her. After a while, James grew tired and quieted himself. She finished her notes and told us she would create a formal evaluation and recommendations, smiled at us, and said, "Thank you for coming."

There was silence in the car driving home. It was as if the three of us knew the outcome would be something we did not want to hear, something that a few therapy sessions, a change in diet, or a round of acupuncture treatments was not going to remedy. A few days after our visit, a packet came in the mail with the evaluation and recommendations.

James was "classically autistic."

Those words were like bullets. I felt them hit me physically. Everything I had feared came rushing in on me. What rolled around in my mind was how many times I had thought, "I can deal with anything but having a handicapped child." This came to me frequently throughout my life when I saw parents pushing a daughter in a wheelchair or carrying a son who could not walk. Now I was the parent I always felt sorry for. "Classically autistic." I was destroyed.

My heart was heavy with this enormously crushing knowledge. Now I knew the reason for James's torment: he was autistic. I accepted it cognitively but I didn't know where to go from there. I began to panic. I didn't know if I could do this.

Star Bright suggested that James come in twice a day, three times a week. These sessions, we read, would not improve him, but they would maintain his current functioning. Without the sessions, he could regress. Regress? Things could get worse? Now we had to figure out a way to pay for sessions that would simply maintain the terrible daily struggles we were experiencing.

I was going to have to educate myself. The beginnings of my research yielded this awful truth: autism has no cure, very little treatment, and virtually no hope. No two autistic kids behave, rage, or interact the same way, and where I lived there were no support groups.

Autism. No cure. Autism. No cure. Autism!

How could there not be an answer? Had no one ever had any success in seeing an autistic child healed? "Please God," I prayed, "Help me find someone who can help us. Tell me there is someone who can help our son."

Tom and I studied autism. The subject is astonishingly broad, falling under a huge umbrella of disorders called Pervasive Developmental Disorder. I now remembered that this was what James's pediatrician had noted as a diagnosis after all of that blood work came back normal. It encompassed everything from attention deficit disorder (ADD) on the really good end, to autism, the really, really bad end. So a Pervasive Developmental Disorder was not a simple thing, not a fixable thing. "How can this be? There's treatment for ADD," I thought. "There's just got to be treatment for autism. There has to be something to help us through this thing we now know by its horrible, frightening name: autism."

I ramped up my daily self-medicinal process—I was drinking to deal with the stress. I had no peace. I didn't sleep well. Alcohol didn't seem to shake off the worries, burdens, and depression that consumed me. We had no support. If your child has cancer, Down syndrome, diabetes—some clearly diagnosable disease or condition—at least there are networks of people to talk to about it. James didn't fall into any of those categories. He was *classically autistic*. I felt like I might go completely insane.

7

NAVIGATING IN FOG

THE TEACHERS AT JAMES's school told me he was improving, but at home I saw none of it. They insisted he was doing well, but at home he was a very different kid. As he got better at school, he seemed to grow worse at home.

As I had begun to learn, autistic children are often extremely book smart. They like the structure of a classroom setting. We couldn't provide that kind of structure at home. It actually seemed normal to me that if he was so intelligent, he would lack some social skills, but it's not just that. Something in his brain was misfiring, making all the connections go haywire. At least this is what the doctors told me about this disorder. The truth is they are still in the dark about so much, and it's one of the reasons we were in the dark. You see, there is no test for autism. There's no autism gene. Blood chemistry won't indicate it, electrolytes remain stable, growths or abnormalities are not visible to verify its presence. It is a diagnosis arrived at after a few hits and a lot of misses. I wondered how anyone could possibly know that autism is a real diagnosis.

What I did know is that no one would sign up for this life. Nobody prays they will have a baby with special needs. But this was *my child*. I couldn't take him to the courthouse to have our mother-son relationship annulled. So I found ways to deal with my pain: I added anti-depressants and anti-anxiety medication to my alcohol regimen.

After a particularly shattering experience with James at a very large church with thousands of members, going to church became something we *used* to do. While sitting in the service of this massive megachurch, I was watching the bingo numbers pop up at the bottom of the big screens.

Well, they were not *really* bingo numbers; let me explain. When parents dropped off their children at the nursery or children's church, they were given a number. When the workers in these vital ministries required a parent, that number would appear at the bottom of the screen. Throughout the service, parents' heads bobbed up and down as they refreshed the memory of their number each time one popped up. If a parent dared ignore their number because they were actually listening to and receiving from the pastor's message, the number began to blink insistently. All around the auditorium, parents' heads would swivel, wondering who was so obtuse they didn't know their number. It made for a service that could not have been much different from the activity of a bingo game. "I-29, I-29... G-12... B-8. Last call for B-8."

I was used to seeing my number every week and knew I was not being summoned because he was about to receive an award for excellent conduct. It could have been for any reason: James was slamming or hitting or screaming; whatever it might be, it was something the nursery workers couldn't handle. You know how church nurseries are. There are no trained professionals. There's rarely ever any training at all for anyone who works in the nursery. They are volunteers. VOLUNTEERS! (A plague God didn't even give the Egyptians: volunteering.) People volunteer for the nursery or for Sunday school mostly because they have to put in time in a ministry. Often having never worked with children in any significant capacity, they end up in rooms with twenty-five kids for an hour and a half, looking for ways to fill the time. And every parent has issues, so the church tried to ensure some procedural structure and prevent lawsuits by providing forms that had to be signed. I had gotten to the point where I signed the forms and said as little as possible so I could get away to the service.

I realized this was dangerous, but the truth is that James was not always and forever unmanageable. Sometimes he got through a service without incident, or without big ones, anyway. Other times, he might be playing quietly, with no indication he was about to erupt, when suddenly, *kaboom*! He did not want to be stuck in a room, coloring a "Jesus wept" picture. He might begin his head-banging exercise. (Here's my number on the screen!) He might go into a tantrum. (Up goes my number.) When I arrived, he might just be lying on the floor, but it all became too much for the volunteers. It got to the point where they would just ask me to take him and go.

I so wanted to start a class on how to manage children with special needs to help train volunteers who worked with children. I didn't do tremendously well with James myself, but I did know more than them. I knew how to quiet him and what might trigger an episode. Surely other special-needs parents could appreciate volunteers at least having some kind of training. But I couldn't get to the pastor. In some of the country's larger megachurches (and even in small, non-mega congregations, sadly), the pastor insulates himself from his members with a layer of administrative pastors who, when they don't want to do something they're not sure of, will defer to the senior pastor. But since you can't get to the senior pastor, you are effectively shut out. I have since decided that I will not attend a church where I cannot speak with my pastor.

I had taken to leaving services ten minutes early, because as we passed the giant Playscape that had been placed for children just off of the lobby, James would start to pull me toward it and soon a fight would ensue. That was a signal for James to blow. So if I left a bit early, I had time to manage the situation and get out of the church without a bunch of people around. And at this point, no longer directing music, my husband and I did not go to services together. I would go to the morning service with James in case we needed to leave and Tom would go to the second service.

This time, I got through the whole service without seeing my number and left my usual ten minutes early to pick him up. I said to the young woman standing at the nursery door, "Hi, I'm James's mom." To my astonishment, the volunteer, whose attention was elsewhere, barely acknowledged me. She just pointed and said, "He's over there," the same way she might have told a sanitation worker, "The trash is in the corner." My son was a *thing* to her. "Take him away," she might as well have said.

James and I made our way down the hall through the mass of people coming out of the sanctuary, having taken a bit longer than usual to get out of the nursery. I asked myself if this was really the place where I was supposed to receive spiritual sustenance—a place where I could not speak to my pastor and where the nursery workers, so unskilled that they began to hate parents because they hated their children, would dismiss me without a word. I felt so ignored and alone I was near tears.

That's when James saw the magical Playscape. He threw himself down on the ground and began to bang his head on the floor so hard I could actually hear his skull bouncing on the tile.

A huge space opened up around me. A man came up and asked, "Do you need some help with him?" What a nice guy, right? If you had heard him, you would not think so. The utter contempt in his voice was chilling. I felt his disgust and disdain. I thought I might be psychic, because I could feel all the people's thoughts directed at me. I knew they believed he needed a spanking because he was out of control. I heard thoughts like, "What is she doing to her child?" and "We're so sick of seeing spoiled children raised by this generation." Cruel, unkind people, coming out of Sunday morning church service.

I looked up at the man and just stared at him as James continued to thrash. I looked at him until he walked away, dripping with distaste.

If James had been in a wheelchair, we would have gotten looks of compassion and many offers of assistance. Because his disability was hidden behind his healthy, blond-haired, blue-eyed, sweet-little-boy appearance, the annoyance on the faces of those walking by was palpable. No one offered a gentle word. They didn't know my son was deathly, deathly ill with no hope for a cure. As I struggled to get James to his feet, I found myself so depleted, so sick with sadness and despair that I wished I could disintegrate right on the spot. I absorbed the unspoken blows, the emotional judgment pouring over me from all who walked by. They didn't know my son was autistic. They couldn't help me even if they did know. No one could help me, and no one would.

That settled church attendance for me.

I was so ashamed. I was ashamed of James. I was ashamed of the kind of mother I was... the kind of mother I was not. If I were a good mother, I would have been able to tell him, "James, stop it right now," and he would stop. I was ashamed of my life, my marriage, my inability to do anything right. The weight of the shame was enormous. I had never had that many witness his outrageous behavior at once.

Our world was getting smaller. The only places Tom and I went were to doctors' offices and the school, where we were called for ARD (Assessment, Review, and Dismissal) meetings. ARDs brought parents, school district representatives, and teachers together to go over goals and the routes to accomplishing them. James would only be assessed and reviewed because the only dismissal that might occur as far as I could see would most certainly be from our home to an institution where he could receive proper care. He would not be dismissed from Special Education.

The goals for James at ARDs were always things like "putting your backpack up when you get to school." Three choices were given for each goal: ongoing, completed, and mastered. As I would glance dully over the list of tasks, I never saw anything James had completed. He'd mastered none of them. In fact, at the very first ARD that Tom and I attended, I pushed to understand the purpose and direction of the regimen of the program. It seemed nothing more than palliative to me. "Is this all you're doing?" I asked. "Is this program just designed to keep him occupied and prevent him from acting out, or is there something else that can be done?" I was looked at as though these were shocking questions, and I couldn't understand why. Didn't they want to tell me? I just wanted to know everything I could.

When we got home, Tom dropped his keys on the table and turned to look at me. "Why did you have to be so hard?" he asked. I was stunned. "Hard?" I responded. "I am trying to find out the very best that can be done for our child. How is that 'hard'? Why don't you have any questions? Don't you want to know what should be happening? Are they doing all they can do and should do?" Tom walked away, waving his hand as though to dismiss me as a hysterical, overwrought mother. He apparently didn't want me to hurt the feelings of people who were supposed to be helping our son.

It was all too much for him. Tom never went to another ARD.

Our marriage was tanking. Tom retreated further into his music instruction, then stayed in his office until nine at night. If I was in serious denial, Tom was completely lost to it. "James will grow out of it," he would say as our son forced himself to throw up if he didn't get what he wanted. "This will pass—stop making such a big deal out of it," he'd sigh as James picked bits of wallpaper off the wall and ate them. "That's your problem. You make a big deal out of everything." He didn't seem to understand, or *want* to understand, that this really was a big deal. Autism was not a head cold.

But as it goes with some people, Tom was simply incapable of accepting what had to be done. I was avoidant but he was profoundly passive, and his passivity was fed by some of his older clients who told him that there was no such thing as autism, that even ADD was a big myth. "We did just fine before there were doctors!" one elderly woman insisted. Because Tom taught children, he saw various behavioral problems and considered James's challenges along the same lines: this is just a behavioral problem that will go away.

Tom's girls would come to visit and it would offer some relief. They'd play with James and it engaged him, and this encouraged Tom's belief that there was some logical explanation for the strange and outrageous actions we witnessed: it was just a phase.

I attended ARDs alone. I felt absolutely isolated and completely stupid. Asking too many questions seemed to bring a chill to the proceedings, so I sat in quiet frustration and despair. I guess the look on my face during these meetings broadcast the fact that I had no hope left. One of the teachers picked up on my desolation. She told me about a pediatric specialist at Scott and White Hospital just outside Austin and suggested I give her a call.

It seemed like a long, long time since I had prayed that God would send someone to help us, and, frankly, I had forgotten I had ever asked. I was willing to try anything, though, so we met with the doctor. She was one of the kindest people I had ever encountered. Tom was still attending doctor appointments with me because he was good at getting James to settle down, and she gently explained to both of us that what we had been told was true: James would be like this for the rest of his life. However, she prescribed something she thought might help: Clonidine, a blood pressure medication. We were to break it up and put it in James's nighttime bottle. This would help to lower his blood pressure just enough that he could relax and enter into REM sleep.

We followed her instructions and for the first time in as long as we could remember, James slept through the whole night instead of waking up at some awful hour and turning on the television full blast. In a world that was always forcing us five steps back, we were able to take one step forward! I was deeply grateful to this woman. She gave us the option of giving James some Clonidine during the day, but I decided that I didn't want him sleepy or groggy at school. Besides, simply getting a full, restful night's sleep put him in a much better frame of mind during the day.

At our next appointment, the doctor told us about a medication that had a remarkable but unreliable effect on autistic children. "It will be a one-in-10,000 shot," she told us, but would be willing to try it if we agreed. There was no hesitation! She had proven herself trustworthy with her first suggestion and I was eager to see if we could make more progress.

She prescribed James a very low dosage of Prozac. We gave it to him the next morning before sending him to school, and sent him along with a long note for the teacher explaining the doctor's work with James.

That afternoon, James came home with a note from his teacher: "James was catatonic and drooled all day." I was heartbroken—I had so wanted this to be a breakthrough. Clearly, our child was not the one-in-10,000 who would be benefiting from this drug. I decided I would not be giving it to him again, but someone at the school apparently felt this was a poor decision. It was most likely easier for everyone when James was drugged up and incoherent, but what occurred next wasn't justified by the circumstances: claim of abuse was once again filed with CPS.

This time CPS didn't even bother to come to the house. A social worker called and said, "Mrs. Mayer, someone is obviously a little trigger happy at the school your son attends. You've been reported for not giving your handicapped child his prescribed medication."

What? I had just been to an ARD meeting! We had discussed goals and commitments and I had explained the strategy of our new doctor, shared our struggles. I thought we were all on the same page. Didn't we all want what was best for James? How could this be happening again?

Even the social worker acknowledged that this report was from someone uninformed about James's condition. CPS had done a full investigation the first time and understood the nature of his illness. But when CPS gets a call, the law says it must investigate. I told her I understood and asked if I could meet with her. She agreed.

8

A CHANGE OF SEASONS

THE FOLLOWING MONDAY MORNING as I walked into the building, guilt washed over me. I hadn't done anything, but the Austin CPS offices were not exactly friendly or welcoming, and probably for good reason. When signing in, a security guard rode with each visitor to the designated floor. Every door had a dead bolt on it because people who are guilty, who really do harm their children, are scary people—hateful, inhuman, unstable people. I was pretty sure those words did not describe me, but it's hard not to feel accused and convicted when walking to a Child Protective Services caseworker's office. Did my child have to be protected from me? I didn't think so, but in my usual emotionally responsive way, by the time I got to where I needed to be I was bordering on hysteria. As I showed the young woman the huge file I had brought, filled with intake forms, school evaluations, doctors' reports, and professional assessments, I explained through my tears that I was trying to do for James what needed to be done. I asked her if she knew about autism.

With a face that looked like she had graduated from college about two hours before I got to her office, I didn't feel good about how she might answer. She didn't disappoint me. "Not really," she said, "but when I was a sophomore I think it was mentioned in a class." I began to sob, making another attempt to explain our situation. To my surprise, she proved to be calm and very professional. "Mrs. Mayer, it is very obvious to us that you and your husband are doing everything in your power to help your child. The fact is we have to call on these reports and there is no way to stop that. We can see without a doubt, on record, that you are doing everything you can." She leaned across her desk and said emphatically, "This is a very unusual circumstance and we are very sorry you have to be put through this."

I left feeling like a blessing had been bestowed on me. How many people got out of a bureaucratic government agency without being misunderstood, whipped around, and feeling like a criminal? This precious caseworker gave me tools and information about autism that I had never received before. She may not have known much about it, but she knew about resources and gave me materials for agencies like Mental Health and Mental Retardation (MHMR) and Any Baby Can, a respite care program for families with special-needs children, and information regarding financial help from Social Security. These agencies offered services like home visits and assistance, assessment services, and more. She asked me a question that nearly knocked me out of my chair: "Didn't your school district tell you about these?"

No, I told her. Why should they?

Because, she responded, these programs are administered by state agencies that work with the school districts to provide some of the services. The schools that administer services have all of this information and should have offered it to me at the very beginning!

I was floored. I called my teacher client who first mentioned the Preparing Preschoolers in Child Development program and told her about my conversation with the caseworker. She, too, was surprised. "The school didn't tell you about any of these services?" she asked me. As we discussed the situation, she explained to me that part of the assessment process the school had to do involved noting the Pervasive Developmental Disorder, Not Otherwise Specified diagnosis from James's pediatrician. This connected with MHMR and its services, which administered the Preparing Preschoolers in Child Development program through a partnership with the Texas Education Association.

But as so often happens when state agencies require schools to provide special- education programs, particularly as they relate to autism, school administrators resist. Frequently the funding to hire skilled teachers and aides may not always be available, or the reorganization of classrooms and workloads is challenging, or the extra work of servicing just one or two children is burdensome. So unless a parent knows to ask specifically about the programs, or is knowledgeable about what is available, the schools will not mention it and will hope the parents never find out.

My teacher client said, "You must say these magic words: 'I want every service that is available to my child.' They are required to comply by offering every service. If you do not say these words, they can claim that you did not request the services and they were thus not obligated to provide them."

This is exactly what had happened. I had not asked for the services by name. I did not know they were available to us, and thus James's school was off the hook.

I was furious. I had been trying so hard for so long to help my child. The school had all of this information and did not share it with me. CPS had to follow up on us twice before we could get information, and we were most likely reported to CPS by an untrained aide who was unfamiliar with the kind of problem their program was supposed to address, which told me the school was most likely not equipped with properly trained aides.

James threw his unique kind of tantrums, but I could throw my own. I went directly to the administration office at his school. I walked in and said loudly to anyone and everyone, "This is going to stop today! If it doesn't stop today, you all are going to build me the most expensive house in town because I am going to sue this place for every last penny you have." The receptionist did what any good receptionist would do: she offered me a beverage.

"No," I said, practically breathing fire, "you are going to find somebody on staff, a school board member, maybe. You are going to find *somebody* right this second. I am not going to leave. If you don't help me today I am going to call every TV station in Texas, stand in front of your little administration building sign out there, and tell them what you have done to me, my family, and my child who cannot speak and is autistic!"

That was all it took. If I had only known that getting mad and acting like I meant business would do something, I would have tried that before becoming my hysterical self. That day, everything got fixed. They found the person who reported us (twice!) to CPS and had a nice long talk with her and assured me that she would be immediately trained in dealing with special-needs children before being allowed back in a classroom. As I demanded "every service that is available to my child" under the jurisdiction of the Texas Education Association, glances were exchanged and nervous assurances were made. I told them I had completely lost faith in their ability to provide the simplest of services which the state had mandated and considered them so far out of compliance that I could not trust them to adequately administer the program.

We came to a mutual decision that the best place for James was at another school in the district in a program called Structured Teaching.

We lived across the street from a school I thought might be the salvation of my son but which turned out to be the source of two uninformed, even cruel, reports to a state agency. It was supposed to be a place I could find some answers but which had withheld valuable information that might have made a tremendous difference in the level of hopeless resignation to which I had been giving in. It was supposed to be a place where professionals knew exactly how to deal with the disorder that plagued my child but which neglected to protect him from someone on staff who was unprofessional enough not to know what autism looked like. I now hated this school. In agreeing to send James to a different school miles from home, I pointed out that since they had failed to perform their duties and had made a very difficult situation exponentially worse, going as far as subjecting my husband and me to possible criminal prosecution, they needed to take care of what they'd created. They agreed to arrange for a bus to pick up James every morning and take him to the new school.

Structured Teaching was a disciplined, very work-oriented, very driven program. Its focus was on improving a child's socialization and behavior enough that at some point, he or she could move into regular classes. I felt good about this approach. I didn't have much faith left in what I had been told at the first school, so perhaps this next experience was what James really, truly needed: a new program, a new school, new teachers, and a clean slate.

Finally, the winds were shifting.

9
PARTLY CLOUDY IN
THE AFTERNOON

JAMES RODE HIS LITTLE bus every morning and actually seemed happy to do it. He qualified for his own full-time aide who cared just for him. (I thought it was because he was just so precious. The truth is, he was so unruly he had to have someone special just for him. There were six other children and they had to monitor him constantly, so an aide was assigned to him permanently.) He had a great time at school with the new kids and brand- new atmosphere. He absolutely loved it. There was so much structure, it met his autistic demands and calmed him. The Clonidine continued to do its work, and I felt like maybe we had turned a corner.

It was home life that was still difficult. We could not provide the structure that James received at school. I had another child I had to take care of, and there was laundry and cleaning to do, pets to take care of, jobs to deal with. Weekends were still especially hard. Because of the great treasure of information the CPS caseworker had given me, we had started to receive some much-needed help, including a monthly check from Social Security, twenty hours a month of respite care from state workers who came to our home to assist with James's needs, and Any Baby Can took him for one Saturday a month. The state also provided for a psychiatric session once a month.

So I couldn't complain; all of this was so much more than we could have imagined after all we had been through. We were deeply grateful to the state of Texas for these wonderful programs; it was unfortunate that it had taken so long to find out about them. The extra help allowed Tom and me to give some time to our daughter. Our marriage, though, was another story.

I was still working, of course, and looking back on it now I don't know how I kept juggling all of these bone-crushing boulders. Work was my refresher and, as I had already discovered, sometimes it turned out to be a source of vitally important information.

Around the time I started to feel like I could breathe a little, one of my clients told me about a ministry team in Plano called Gospel Revelations Ministries (GRM), which specialized in setting people free from the bondage of the stresses and strains of life. I wasn't quite sure what that meant, but I did know that I wasn't acquiring the appropriate skills to raise a handicapped child. I wondered if I should do a whole life inventory and repent to God, make amends, do whatever was needed to do to get myself right so that I could raise this special-needs little boy and still be a mother to special, beautiful Paige. It wouldn't hurt to also get some help for my marriage, which suffered from the stresses and strains of my failures, of James, of our inadequate ways of approaching all of it. Hearing about this ministry created an urgency within me, and I felt I had to connect with it.

The team from GRM came to Austin in March of 1999 for a meeting at the home of a supporter. In my usual over-the-top excitement and expectation, I decided that if I could just get there, God would do something miraculous in me to make me a great mother. I would walk out of that place ready for whatever was to come. The Lord would help me walk through this and give me whatever I needed to raise James.

That didn't happen, but I did discover I could schedule an appointment to be seen. The first available opening was four months away. I took it, and thanked God every night—until my July appointment—that He was sending me to godly people who would help me.

My ministry date finally came. I didn't know anything about personal ministry, in spite of all of the church work I had been involved in. As I have said before, it's easy in the church world to pass for being very spiritual. Outward appearances can be deceptive—even to oneself. I was in church all the time, I had a husband who knew everything about the Bible (which translated to knowing everything about God), I had been to India to preach the gospel, I had even prayed occasionally. All that meant I was Christian, right? It meant I was different from someone who *wasn't* a believer, right?

Actually, for all I knew about what it meant to be a follower of Christ, I was about as Christian as any clueless nonbeliever on the street. I had some knowledge, but it was not life-transforming knowledge. I knew who Jesus was, but I didn't know Him with any intimacy—the deep, personal connection that gives a believer the awareness of the Lord's presence and activity in one's life. I didn't really hook up with God in prayer. I just knew I was supposed to pray to Him, as opposed to, say, Shu, the Egyptian god of air.

So I thought what was going to happen with the folks from GRM might be something like EST training from the 1970s. I would write down my sins and put them in a coffee can and bury it. I could clear everything up and be the world's greatest mother of a handicapped child. I had no idea what would happen. I was ready for anything.

I arrived at a church where signs pointed to a Sunday school room. Six Gospel Revelation Ministry workers were there, each appointed to do different things. There were those praying quietly, providing an atmosphere of intercession and expectation. Others sat with a Bible, gathering specific scriptures for me as the session progressed. It began with a collection of my life history, the whole how-did-you-get-here personal tour. There was even a personality test. The team wanted to know me as much as possible.

Sheila Ramsey, who heads up the ministry, then took a look at the information gathered and talked with me about the level of fear and anger with which I approached life; how much of my "adult" sensibilities ruled my "child" reactions; and other things. She walked through my life with me, looking at my foundational experiences, determining how I operated spiritually. This led her to take a look at experiences that had opened a door for strongholds to take root in my life: what had happened to me and what I had done to myself; how I had contributed to my own dysfunctions and allowed the enemy to settle into areas of my mind and heart. She surveyed my entire internal landscape.

As Sheila and I discussed my issues, the Lord gave her specific actions for me to take. She wrote on a yellow legal pad as we talked. The team helped her by praying and offering the scriptures they felt the Holy Spirit was giving them. This part alone took a couple of hours, and I was impressed with how thorough everyone was. This was serious stuff!

After some time, she began giving me instruction regarding things I needed to do with James. She told me first to begin playing Christian music in my home around the clock, and especially in his room as he slept. She said the enemy attacks children when they are infirm or asleep. I don't know if I completely understood at that time who "the enemy" was, but I was receiving an education on the insidious ways the devil worked against the children of God. She told me to pray for my child every night. I had never done that, and I felt like I had been missing something as she spoke to me. (*Wow—I should pray for my child! Of course!*) She told me to anoint him with oil and gave me steps on how to pray, taking me through the basic tools; how to put on the full armor of God, like it says in Ephesians 6:10–18. I don't know how many times I had read it, how many times I had heard the passage quoted, but it was as though my eyes were seeing light after being in dark, solitary confinement for a long time. I knew what she was telling me was right. It was completely foreign to anything I had ever seen or heard, but it just lit up with truth.

Everything Sheila was giving me was like water to a dying, thirsty person. If what she was telling me had been spoken in church, I must have missed it entirely. I knew it was not to be taken lightly. She told me, "The responsibility is yours now. Pray with conviction: 'I break every evil thing that is attached to my child, my husband, my life.' You have truth now," she said, "and you can do this." Somehow, wonderfully, I got it. It wasn't about knowing every last scripture in the Bible and putting on a church face and acting like what I thought a Christian should act like. It was about being able to live.

Then things got a bit tougher. Sheila told me I had to ask forgiveness of my parents for being a rebellious and difficult adolescent. *Whoa!* Put on the brakes! As we talked about my past and got to some of the hidden parts of my life, a whole lot of pain popped up. This was not just a sweet little prayer session I was in; it was a gut-wrenching, heart-wringing profession of all the resentment and hatred and self-deception I had managed all of my life. I saw that the paths I had chosen and the choices I had made were all my own, without the guidance of the Lord.

My life was not something I really wanted to look back on. Making a full review of what I had done and how I had gotten through was like a pile of old coats I had stuffed in a closet until workers from The Salvation Army could come by and pick them up: I knew they were there, but they were out of sight, and they were not worth my attention anyway. The truth is I had a past, and it wasn't pretty. I haven't revealed everything here; perhaps I'll be ready to do that one day, but not at this writing. What I can tell you is that I have had some shameful episodes in my life. My story didn't begin with my return to Austin on a plane from Los Angeles; it started long before with sinful reactions to less-than-loving messages received in childhood, with boomerang-like responses that were so foolish they defy explanation. I have been blessed (and cursed!) with a personality that was exemplified in Margaret Mitchell's great literary character Scarlett O'Hara: as long as I can figure out a way forward, I'll think about yesterday later. I'll think about the residue I'm creating when I'm comfortable and safe. The ends will justify the means, because I need to get to the place where I'm protected against all unkind, unloving forces that want to destroy my hope for happiness. I will manipulate and fix and negotiate and demand until I can force life into the comfortable pattern that my deepest heart cries for. Never mind that I ignore all warning signs and push others into uncomfortable positions of submission to my emotional displays. I need to be safe. I need to be in control. I need to be loved.

Until that day I had no idea how much God loved me and wanted me to walk in the freedom *He* has to offer. I didn't want to look truthfully at myself, because I already knew what was underneath my bubbly, smiling exterior; I preferred exteriors to interiors anyway. I was desperately seeking freedom, but I didn't think the Lord had much to do with that. The freedom I sought was liberation from the terrorizing truth that I was not good enough to be loved or accepted, and so I performed many acts of dignity-destroying self-hatred in an attempt to purge myself of my greatest fear.

The freedom I was offered that day was accessible to everyone, and especially to me. With a child who could not function normally, a marriage as hollow as a chocolate bunny sitting on a drugstore shelf at Easter time, and a heart so heavy I felt like the floor could not support my weight, I wondered if I was ever going to be allowed to be at peace inside. Surely all of what I was experiencing was the punishment of a God who had seen my rotten life and was giving me what I deserved. Secretly, I agreed I deserved affliction but while I was going through it I sought remedies; none of them were lasting and I was exhausted beyond description.

In a moment of clarity ("Oh, *this* is what we were singing about in church all the time!") I just stopped. I quit acting. I stood still and listened, and I heard the Lord Jesus tell me He loved me. And I believed Him, and from that point on nothing was the same.

At the end of our time together, having heard what we were going through as a family with James and his condition, Sheila reached over and touched my arm. She said, "I believe we can take James through ministry so he can be healed from autism."

I had been through hours of healing ministry with the team that day, and I was ready to do anything, but this was beyond me. The suggestion that James could be healed was outrageous. I didn't laugh in her face, but in my mind I did one of those "spit shots" the guests on Johnny Carson's late-night show used to do when, just after taking a sip of water, Johnny would make some insanely funny comment and that sip went flying all over the furniture in a reaction that couldn't be contained. I knew healing from autism wasn't a possibility. If there were healing for autism, it would have been all over *Parade Magazine*, *60 Minutes*, or featured on *The Oprah Winfrey Show*. After all of the wonderful ministry I had received, I didn't want to appear ungrateful, so I just kept my mouth shut, but I found her suggestion ludicrous.

Then she said, with what had to be perfectly good intentions, "The ministry will be praying and waiting on God to see when to take James through deliverance." I had heard things like this so many times in church without understanding what "deliverance" meant. I was deeply skeptical, but I was also desperate for something that would take my child out of his misery, something that would be the answer to a healthy family and some semblance of a peaceful home. I felt I did not have time to wait, but I was going to have to do first what I had been instructed to do and go from there.

I must admit, though, that I was stopped dead in my tracks by Sheila's insistence that I go to my parents and ask their forgiveness. There was so much difficulty in just wrapping my mind around the need for it. Because Gospel Revelation Ministry was in town for several days, Sheila invited me to bring my parents for an appointment so that I would have help in taking this step.

Going to see them with the intention of forgiveness was enormously difficult. I told them about GRM, the ministry I had received, and explained that I wanted to take the actions meant to set things right in my life. They listened, and were willing to do anything I thought might help, so just a few days later, they came with me to the same Sunday school room.

It was not pretty. As my mother and father brought up some issues they'd had with me, all of my old patterns flared up. My pain sent me on a tear and I became obnoxious and disrespectful. I berated them for all of my perceived hurts. I wanted explanations and reasons. For that session, instead of keeping the focus on *me*, on what I had contributed to our relationship, on asking for their forgiveness, I made it about them. Did they make mistakes raising me? Yes, and I wanted them to say they were sorry about every last thing. I wanted *them* to make everything right.

It was not a productive session. My anger and resentment drove them right out of the room. They got up and left.

As I sat there sobbing out my bitterness, Sheila spoke quietly. "I have never seen anything like that," she said. There was a long silence. "Go apologize to them." I looked up at her, knowing she was right but dreading what had to be done. I asked if I could just call them. She became indignant with me, just what I needed. "Do you want your child healed or not?" she said emphatically. "Honor your father and mother. Grow up. Humble yourself under the mighty hand of God and there will be results."

I wanted His kingdom to come and His will to be done in my house and in the life of my child. I drove out to the house and apologized and asked my parents to forgive me.

Sheila had told me to play Christian music all the time, but in particular to play it softly in James's room while he was sleeping. She said sometimes kids are tormented the most while trying to sleep, and this made sense to me, knowing how tortured James would act at night. The very first night I implemented this simple strategy, along with praying for James as he lay in his bed, there was a huge difference. He became noticeably peaceful, more than I had ever seen before.

I was very green at all of this. I had been a church worker for a long time but this was something altogether different than being a church person. Through continuing sessions while they were in town, the Gospel Revelation Ministry team was teaching me what it meant to be a follower of Jesus. I was grateful for this ministry, grateful for Sheila, grateful that I had one more strategy to help me with my ongoing battle. I was beginning to feel that maybe I could start to be the mother I always knew I could be.

I asked Tom if he would come with me to a session Gospel Revelation Ministry would facilitate for us. His deep avoidance kicked in and he told me he didn't need "some woman" praying for him or his kid. But I did. I needed whatever I could get. Tom wouldn't go to any of my remaining sessions. After all we had been through, I wondered if my marriage was completely dead.

I didn't have to wonder much longer. The very next month, I made a decision to have radical prophylactic mastectomies. For generations back in both lines of my family, breast cancer has claimed women. I had done a great deal of reading and put a lot of thought into this very severe preventative measure, and I decided I would rather be sure that I would be around to take care of my children than wait and hope that breast cancer didn't show up to take me far too early. I might go some other way, but at least I could fight proactively against a very real threat.

Here was the dead marriage confirmation: Tom did not go with me to my doctor's appointments. His whole response to my decision was a big shrug. He didn't seem the least bit concerned that I was undergoing major surgery in which serious body parts would be removed. We had become a married couple living like two single people in the same house: we each had our own sched-ules, our own routines, our own worlds. The only thing that kept us connected was our children. I felt deeply sad, and went into a nine-hour surgery knowing we were over.

As drastic as the surgery was, I wasn't upset by it. The fear of cancer had been a pestering little monkey on my back. I just felt relieved it was done and behind me, and moved on with reconstructive surgery.

To my surprise, members of the Gospel Revelation Ministry team called me in October to see how I was doing and if I had been addressing the issues we had discussed. I told them about my surgery and they were stunned. "Why didn't you call us for prayer?" they cried. I was dumbfounded. I could have called? I could have called and had prayer! I didn't know! I was completely childlike. I didn't even think of having someone else pray for me.

As we talked, they told me they had continued to pray for God to talk to them about the time for James's deliverance. I was shocked. I had never heard of someone praying for someone and then waiting in expectation for an answer! What they modeled for me was *standing*. They prayed and stood firm on the promise that God would answer—in His wise timing, not according to their demands. I thought you prayed and if things didn't happen, too bad. To stand and stick with it was new to me.

James was undeniably better, but he was still not fully manageable. As effective as the suggestions given to me by the folks at GRM were, James was still autistic. He was getting bigger and was physically becoming much harder to control. I knew that we were not far from having to start looking for an appropriate institutional setting. I wasn't going to learn to be the perfect mother of a special-needs child overnight, and that's what he needed: overnight change. Between the diagnoses, the schools, the agencies, and the ministry—each had helped in its own way during the past four and a half years—I had to admit a sobering conclusion: even with everything that was suggested, with everything implemented, every little bit of improvement and movement toward success, none of it was enough. It was unbearable to think about, but it was life. James was not going to get better, and there would come a point when I could not stop him from hurting himself or anyone else, perhaps even Paige. As I had with so many other things in my life, I could not manipulate, persuade, or maneuver my way out of this.

And then, as all good stories go, the phone rang.

10

I CAN SEE CLEARLY NOW

I T WAS JANUARY, AND the administrator for GRM was calling. I hadn't heard from them since October. I honestly thought I never would. I was pleased they'd given me some tools that made a difference with James, and certainly my own life was making a turnaround: I was praying every day, I had a newfound relationship with God, I was excited. I felt like I had gotten more than I had dreamed I could from my experience with them. To my astonishment, I was informed the team had been praying and felt that it was now time to take James through ministry.

I was speechless. I honestly did not think they were going to call. Oh, I know—they had reminded me just three months before of their continuing prayer and expectation, but I kept being surprised that they were actually praying for *me*, specifically. It was still all uncharted territory for me. I was also a little frightened by this news. What was "taking James through ministry" going to entail? I had watched people in church pray and carry on about all kinds of things that never seemed to show any real results as far as I could see. I didn't want that for my boy. I didn't want it for myself. I couldn't take a big buildup with a tremendous letdown. I would rather find a caring, competent setting for James and place him where he would be properly looked after than allow my hopes to be pumped up and then hopelessly dashed by well-meaning people.

But I thought about how thorough GRM had been with me, how carefully they approached my situation. I thought about how they had followed up to see how I was doing. These were people who seemed to honestly care about me. I wanted to trust them.

So I took the first opening they had. The following month Tom, James, and I met the ministry team at a nearby church. As we walked into the sanctuary and I saw Sheila and the other ministry workers, I could not hold back my tears. Sheila asked me why I was crying and I told her it was because I was afraid. I was terrified this was not going to work and would end up being some kind of cruel joke.

She gave me a stern look. "I beg your pardon," she said, "God said James is going to be healed!" She spoke with such authority I almost took a step back. It dried my tears right up. OK, who am I to argue with God? My perspective was instantly changed.

We sat down. The folks on the team began asking probing questions, and Tom and I were soon explaining our most challenging struggles with our son and how we responded to his tantrums. James was sitting on the floor by a wall, rocking, locked in his autistic world. He had no idea why we were there and he soon began making it obvious he was ready to go: he started hitting his head on the wall.

Sheila crouched next to him and spoke to him softly, asking him to say, "Jesus is Lord." He tried. He wasn't proficient with language, not even close to where he should be for his age, but he responded to her and attempted to repeat the words. She patted him as she got up to take her seat, and observed him, taking notes on her yellow pad. Tom and I didn't utter a sound; only the ministry workers prayed in low tones. I felt like I was in a very holy place. I wondered if Tom could feel it.

Suddenly, Sheila announced it was time to pray for James. She instructed Tom to pick him up and hold him on his lap and explained that everyone was going to place their hands on him and pray together. As Tom went and lifted him up, James expressed his unhappiness in a visible way. *Thrashing* might be the word to describe it—yes, *thrashing* pretty much says it all. But Tom was used to this behavior and was able to hold him close as the team members and I gathered around to gently touch him. As we laid hands on him and prayed, Sheila named a demonic spirit and said—I remember this specifically—that it would "have to go into the dry places in Jesus' name." At that very moment, James threw his arm back and started screaming at the top of his lungs: "Come back! Come back! Come back, come back, come back!"

It was the wail of someone losing something, a desperate plea filled with fear and abandonment. James had never spoken those words before, and certainly never as clearly, being speech impaired and barely able to communicate. His ways of making his wishes known were grunts and hysterical, wild behaviors that we had learned to decipher. Now he was reaching for something as though he could feel it leaving his presence, demanding articulately: "Come back!"

Tom and I were in complete and utter shock. The hair on my arms stood up and the room was completely silent. Something *was* leaving him: something that had kept him oppressed for so many years, that had kept him imprisoned, feeding like a parasite on his innocence and joy until he wasn't a little boy anymore, but a tormented, tortured, animalistic being.

After a moment, James pulled his arm back and settled down, instantly compliant. He actually seemed sleepy. Tears were pouring from my eyes as I considered that a spiritual presence with the intent of keeping my child trapped in a hellish existence had kept us fooled for so long. I didn't know. I didn't understand spiritual things. I didn't know I could pray and expect answers—positive answers, blessings that were promised to me in scripture. I thought other people had power. The deacons had power. The pastor had power. I didn't know that I had power. I didn't understand the value of the sacrifice of my Savior. I didn't know He'd hung on the cross to give me something to work with. I wanted to be able to pray with power. I had never seen effectual prayer like I had just witnessed. My life was changed forever in that moment.

We prayed for a bit longer, and Sheila said we were done. Tom and I were given an appointment for the next session. "We're not done," Sheila told us. "This was quite dramatic, but it is not over." She told us that James might display the same behaviors, but we were to speak to him using the name of Jesus, reminding him that he was free. She told us not to be afraid; no being that had been comfortable in its role as James's tormentor was going to want to stay away, and James only knew how to respond the ways he'd grown used to. She reminded me to play his music at night, anoint him with oil, and continue to pray. "Don't think this is over," she said again. "The enemy is still working against your child. Don't think he won't tantrum. You continue to pray specific prayers of protection," and she gave me examples.

Sheila turned to Tom with a stern admonition. "You are the head of the household and you are his father. The change that will come over your child will not stick unless you come for some deliverance yourself." He was silent.

As we got back in the car, Tom and I sat for a while as James blinked his sleepy eyes. We had never seen, experienced, or even heard of anything like we had just witnessed. I realized that something profound had happened, and I now had a responsibility—a deep responsibility—to accept what I had seen and heard and put it to work. We drove home in silence.

James was immediately calmer. He was more manageable. We sensed a change in his basic nature, and I don't quite know how else to explain that. We could simply tell something had changed. From that day, James was different. I'm not talking about the kind of "different" Clonidine yielded, or the "different" that resulted from a rigorous and structured school program. It wasn't like the little fixes we'd had previously. This was a complete turnaround.

Sheila was right, though—there were residual behaviors. James did tantrum. He did pound his head or do his thrashing number, but they seemed—I don't know—less powerful, like the wind had been taken out of his sails. I would begin to pray as I picked him up, thanking the Lord that James was free no matter what I saw. Little by little, his energy for destructive activity dissipated, even though there were flair-ups.

One day, James pulled a tantrum, and I practiced the

prayers I had been told to pray. He didn't respond right away and as I struggled with him, I started to lose my temper. I thought back to the session at the church, and I raised my voice over his shouting and declared, "I bind this thing in Jesus' name!"

James became a wild man. He wasn't having any of that, and in a moment he was nearly overpowering me physically. I breathed desperate prayers, instinctively asking God to forgive me, once again thanking God for James's freedom and for the peace of the Holy Spirit. As I got him settled, I realized with tremendous clarity that I had simply mimicked what I had witnessed. I didn't yet fully understand what it meant to pray in the name of Jesus. I was clueless to the whole praying thing, and I somehow knew I had overstepped my bounds.

I called GRM immediately and discussed the incident with a couple of the prayer team members. They encouraged me and told me to continue praying as I had been instructed. Essentially, they explained that it was dangerous to antagonize what you don't know how to deal with. "The enemy is smart and calculated and organized," I was told. "You think he doesn't know you? He's taking advantage of your ignorance. You don't use the name of Jesus lightly. You use it with knowledge and power." I had a lot to learn.

Tom could not deny the obvious change in James. He called GRM to sign up for personal ministry. I heard him on the phone: "I want my boy to have this." He had seen the reality of this kind of ministry and now he wanted it for himself. He realized he had some baggage, too.

We had three more sessions with the GRM ministry team over the next fourteen weeks, each one producing exponential change in James's cognition and behavior. By June of 2000, he completed the prayer and deliverance sessions that changed his life. For four and a half years James had been in a closet of autistic bondage. After ministry, he was like an uncaged bird. His mind seemed to change daily. He developed quickly in areas we had thought were unrecoverable. His growth was—and continues to be—remarkable.

James is now fourteen years old and in the eighth grade. To look at him today, you would never know how tortured and violent, how inhuman he had once behaved. He is a sweet, well-spoken, quiet, respectful, loving boy, on his way to being what was originally planned for him. He is on the football and basketball teams at school and the city bowling league. He attends Special Education classes for catch-up in language, reading, and writing; and he's in regular classes for all other areas, with inclusion assistance.

This is something only God can do. This is bigger than what the medical field could promise or state agencies manage or those with good intentions assist. It is called a miracle.

James is not the only one who has been playing catch-up. I, too, have been hungrily absorbing what I had been blind to for years. I grew up reading the Bible, and even when playing church, I knew what the Bible said. I thought it was just a book with some great stories—and for me, they were just that: *stories.* But they are far more than simple accounts of events. Jesus was showing us the power that those who believe in Him and follow His commandments have access to today. Not just long ago and far away; not available only to the super-spiritual or the biblically educated elite; today, in the 21st century, among normal folks like you and me His power is available. My child is living proof that there are some things far bigger than we can explain that require a God far greater than we've ever been told about.

Not every autistic child is demonically possessed, but autism is a curse. In that sense, it must be seen as an oppressive and tormenting force that must be faced with more than just the standard social service tools. The enemy of God wants the people of God ignorant and in despair; this is the ultimate curse. But the Father is in the curse-busting business, and so whether He leads us to phenomenally gifted physicians and clinicians, or to alternative therapies, or to those who know how to address spiritual matters in the power of the blood of the Lord Jesus Christ of Nazareth, He wants us to be free. He wants our children to be free.

NOW WHAT?

I N MARK 5, JESUS meets a man who is possessed by demons and He calls them out. The demons head into a herd of pigs that promptly run off a cliff, and the man is freed of their torment. He is so grateful to be well and whole that he begs Jesus for the opportunity to go with Him and serve Him. But Jesus tells him he cannot. Instead, he is instructed to do two things: First, go and tell everyone he knows of what the Lord has done for him; and second, to tell them the Lord had mercy and compassion on him.

I am here to tell every person in every nation that the Lord wants to heal and show His compassion. His miracle-working, healing power is accessible to us all. *All of us!* Everyone single one of us! You can trust Him. Nothing about today catches God by surprise; nothing about your experience hits Him from left field. Bring everything to Him and see what He will do.

The effects of the terrible condition James and his father and I lived through were almost unbearable. God reached in and gave us a way out of that hell. I never want to forget what He did for me and for my family, and

I will share James's story for the rest of my life. There are tens of thousands of families who go through this same kind of experience every day and they have no hope. I want you to know there is a Healer and giver of hope: His name is Jesus.

Jesus came to this earth as a man and died from an agonizing form of capital punishment for the sins of every human being in the world. It was His desire that those He died for would live in an abundance of joy and fruitfulness of spirit. Christ hung on a cross as a curse so we would not have to live with unrelenting problems like sickness and mental defects and emotional torment. "By his wounds we are healed," says the Isaiah 53:5, and I believe that. By the beatings He took, we obtained healing. I want everyone to know that what is accessible to us, is available for all those who believe in Him.

When the doctor told me, "Your child has autism and there is no hope or chance that he will ever get better," I heard it but I didn't fully believe it. There are some of you who are holding this book right now and you know in your heart that the words, "There is no hope or chance he will get better" is a lie. It is not the truth. There is truth that is accepted here, in this earthly dimension, and then there is a truth we can't see but we know exists. It is the truth of God's kingdom. Remember how Jesus said, "My kingdom is not of this world" (John 1:36)? The truth in that kingdom is truer than anything you will ever hear from those on this earth with even the best of intentions.

Pray and ask God to reveal to you that truth. That truth will bypass your understanding and become the seed of hope in your life. I know that hope is real. I am not unusual. This is not a fantasy. James's story could be anyone's story. It could be your story.

TO CONTACT THE AUTHOR

Karen@KarenMayer.org